ACCESSING
English
GRAMMAR

for
teachers of English
as a second language

FEROOZ AFSHAR

CONTENTS

This book is dedicated to all the teachers and students

who put up with my experimentation

— and those who didn't.

And

A very special thanks to

DAVID WEHNER

for his meticulous advice and eye.

INTRODUCTION

If you've picked up this book out of curiosity you have already taken the first step to becoming an involved teacher of ESL.

The purpose of this grammar book is to provide a simple, succinct and overall view of the way English grammar works. It is primarily aimed at teachers of English as a second language, to be used as a quick guide to understanding and explaining the general concepts contained in the language. Learners of the English language might also benefit from the simplicity of this presentation. The book's aim is to provide ordinary, everyday English as simply as possible.

At the onset I have to say, my experience in teaching English Grammar has been that there is no such thing as grammar as we understand it. In the sense that no grammatical rule can be used ad infinitum *without arriving at an exception and being asked that very difficult question, '**Why** is it this way?' What we have are conventions; the way language is manipulated, so the answer to that question can only be 'This is how it's done.'*

*The idea came about after years of teaching and in consultation with other teachers of English as a second language – and being consulted. There are plenty of very good books on English grammar, but I have often heard teachers express frustration at the complex and wordy ways in which some very simple concepts are explained. I have attempted to remove the complexity and present the more common aspects of the grammar in a visual manner. I have taken the position that grammar can be explained by the position of the word rather than 'rational' explanation. 'Location, location, location,' as real estate agents would say. Consider these two sentences: I **work** eight hours a day. I like **work**. The word **work** is the same but the different positions change the function of the word; learners of English need to understand this.*

The book contains five parts. Part 1 is an overall linear view of the structure of English sentences, consisting of the declarative, imperative, exclamatory and interrogative forms. These sentences have been set out in an immediate and dynamic format. Part 2 consists of the parts of speech, their position and function. Part 3 elaborates and provides further explanation of the parts of speech. Part 4, Other grammatical structures, contains structures essential to the English language, such as Conditional sentences, Relative clauses and phrases, Question formation, Phrasal verbs, etc. Part 5 *provides exercises that begin with the general 'fill- the-gap' type provided in most English language textbooks and workbooks and moves on to involve the reconstruction of whole sentences of a more complex nature. These exercises are intended to make the learner **think** about how sentences in English are constructed. They encourage the learner to look at the whole sentence.*

I'd love to say this is the definitive work on English grammar (I doubt if ever there can be such a work on language); nevertheless, I hope it will provide an easier entré *into understanding and explaining how English is formed.*

Treat this book as providing pathways into the forest that the English language is, and as pathways in forests often tend to do; you are likely to be led astray; in which case you might need to backtrack and choose a different path.

If at any point I seem adamant in the rightness of my approach, treat that with a bit of sc(k)epticism/salt! My theory is:

> Language is correct when what is transmitted
> and what is understood are relatively similar.

And I say this because language is always evolving; it is absorbing, challenging, simplifying and complicating.

English, like other languages, has become a borderless entity; there is nothing that can stop it from being infiltrated by other languages. Here, in Aotearoa/New Zealand, Maori words such as: **Kia Ora, whanau, koha** *etc., are already a part of everyday English.*
We might ponder on this:

> One man's meat is another man's *poisson.*

Some of what I say may raise eyebrows, but, hey!

HOW TO GET THE BEST
OUT OF THIS BOOK

Part 1
A linear anatomy of the English sentence

This section gives an overall picture of how English sentences are constructed. It is an easy, ready reference pointing out what the subject, verb and object (completion) segment of each sentence consists of. While this part looks daunting at first glance, a careful study of this section will show that it contains almost all one would need to teach, or to learn, the language.

It provides a ready chart of the four forms of English sentences mentioned in the introduction.

Part 2
Parts of speech

The Parts of speech section provides the types and some of the words that go to form the parts of speech and the full range of tenses (aspects). It has deliberately been kept to as few words as possible to enable the reader to understand and apply the concept without unnecessary complexity.

The columns differentiate the characteristics of each part of speech which help the reader to pinpoint what one might be looking for. If for instance one wants to know what the auxiliary verbs actually are, they need only look at the auxiliary section and the full array of these verbs are provided: where they are located in the sentence; how they function and finally there are sample sentences to enable one to see them in 'action'.

Part 3
Explanation to Parts of speech

This section goes a bit further in explaining the uses and functions of each part of speech. It provides nuances and idiosyncrasies that these parts might contain. For instance, I have put Causative verbs with the Auxiliary verbs because they seem to share a similarity and put Stative verbs with present continuous to point out that not all verbs can function as a continuous verb.

So if Conjunctions in Part 2 is compared with Conjunctions in Part 3, one will easily see that while the explanation in the Part 2 is adequate, Part 3 gives a more satisfying presentation. The reader has a choice: settle for Part 2 or read on.

Obviously, there are going to be grey areas; in which case find other sources to satisfy your opinion. The present perfect is one case in mind; 'shall' as an impertive is another: "Cinders! You shall go to the ball.", etc.

Part 4
Other grammatical structures

In this section I have put in those structures that don't 'exactly' fit into what I understand as 'grammar'. These are whole structures, such as Conditional sentences and Relative sentences which have a style of their own as do the different ways questions are formed.

Part 5
Exercises

I am not a fan of gapfill exercises. Having observed students doing these exercises and then being unable to reproduce the full sentence has put me off gapfill exercises. However, in keeping with the propensity for languages to provide anomalies, I have produced my own: I have begun each exercise with a gapfill.

If each one of us lived alone on an isolated, uninhabited island from the day we appeared on earth, we would have no need for language. Language, as we well know, is a communicative tool. Students should be encouraged to work as teams. Each exercise is a communicative device encouraging students to share their knowledge. Teaching is the best way to learn; if a student can explain a concept, they are well on the way to learning it. Then, of course, there is the lone-wolf learner – leave them alone and they'll come home bringing their knowledge with them.

Each exercise has a mixture of simple and complex structures; this mixture does three things: it shows the students what they know and what they need to learn, and when they solve something outside their experience they feel empowered. My experience has been that complex exercises enable students to develop a more concrete understanding of what they have learnt.

These exercises may be utilized in any order depending on the level being taught. Feel free to copy them; however, writing one's own exercises that suit the needs of the class could be more satisfying for both teachers and students.

I make, yes make, my students write the exercises in their notebooks. They first discuss the exercise, sentence by sentence, and when they have got the construction right; they consolidate it by writing the sentences in their notebooks. They 'hate' it, but there you are! So discuss, solve, write.

SUGGESTED READING

Azar, B. S. (1999) *Understanding and Using English Grammar* (3rd Ed). NY, U.S.A. White Plains

Celce-Murcia, M. & Larsen-freeman, D. (1998) *The Grammar Book: An ESL/EFL Teachers Course* (2nd Ed). Boston, U.S.A. Cengage Learning.

Crystal, D. (2006) *The Cambridge Encyclopedia of the English Language* (2nd Ed). Cambridge, UK. CUP. Collins Cobuild (Ed. Sinclair, J.) (1997) *English Grammar.* London, UK. HarperCollins.

Leech, G. Cruikshank, B. & Ivanič, R. (1998) *An A-Z of English Grammar & Usage.* Essex, UK. Longman. Parrott, M. (2010) *Grammar for English Language Teachers* (2nd Ed). Cambridge, UK. CUP.

Quirk, R. & Greenbaum, S. (1975) *A University Grammar of English.* London, UK. Longman. Swan, M. (1992) *Practical English Usage.* Oxford, UK. OUP.

Thornbury, S. & Underhill, A. (2005) *Uncovering Grammar.* London, UK. MacMillan.

Trask, R. L. (2000) *The Penguin Dictionary of English Grammar.* London, UK. Penguin Books.

PART 1

A linear anatomy of the English sentence

A LINEAR ANATOMY OF THE ENGLISH SENTENCE

The basic Active sentence consists of		
a subject	**a verb**	**and usually a complement which might contain one or more objects.**
The subject consists of	**The verb consists of**	**The complement consists of**

adjectives   adj
adverbs   adv
conjunctions   con
articles (definite)   dart
(indefinite)   iart
abstract nouns   an
proper nouns   PN
common nouns   cn
     singular; plural   sg;pl
     countables   ct
     uncountables   uct
pronouns   pn
     singular; plural   sg;pl
gerunds   g
possessive pronouns   psn
     singular; plural   sg;pl
demonstrative adjective   dadj
     singular; plural   sg;pl
prepositions   pr
time phrases   tphr
place phrases   phr
relative pronouns   rpn
and (relative) clauses   rcl
These can be combined in an infinite variety of constructions. See charts below.
	the tenses (aspects):
	Present simple prs
	Present continuous prc
	Present perfect pp
	Present perfect continuous ppc
	Past simple pts
	Past continuous ptc
	Past perfect ptp
	Past perfect continuous ptpc
	Future f
	Assisting (helping) verbs
	Auxiliary verbs av
	Modals m
	Semi-modals sm
		everything the subject has. However, some *pronouns change into their object form.*
		
		Pronouns:

Pronouns:

subject	object
I	**me**
You	you
He	**him**
She	**her**
They	**them**
We	**us**
It	it

DECLARATIVE SENTENCES

Active sentences.
Italics: actual grammar (parts of speech).
Bold: actual words.
See page 18 for explanation of parts of speech

subject	verb	object (completion)
iart+cn	*prs(be-verb)*	*iart+sgctcn*
A+dog	**is**	**an+animal.**
PN	*pts(be-verb)*	*art+adj+sgctcn*
Peter	**was**	**a+good+actor.**
dart+sgctcn+pr+dadj+sgctcn	*prc (3rd personsg)*	*(adj+sgctcn). (tphr)*
The+teacher+of+this+class	**is+leaving**	**(next+week).**
PN	*ptc*	*con+dart+sgctcn+pts+sgpsn +sgctcn.*
Peter	**was sleeping**	**when the cat ate his burger.**
dart+sgctcn+rpn+(clause)	*ppc(3rd personsg)*	*adv+pr+(iart+adj+ucctcn). (tphr)*
The+man+who+ (is teaching us)	**has been living**	**here+for+(a+long+time).**
sgpsn+ plctcn	*modal Negative+base verb*	*pl psn+ uctcn*
Her+students	**couldn't+do**	**their+homework.**
past tphr,+1st person	*pts*	*pr+PN+pr+sgpsn+sgctcn*
Two years ago,+I	**went**	**to+Spain+with+my+wife.**
sgpsn+sgctcn	*pts*	*pr+PN+pr+sgpn+(past tphr)*
My+wife	**went**	**to+Spain+with+me+ (two years ago).**
plpn+sm	*prs (base verb)*	*dadj+sgctcn+adv*
They+want to	**buy**	**that+house+soon.**
1st person pn	*ppc*	*pr+g+dadj+sgctcn*
I	**have been thinking**	**about leaving this country.**
plpn	*modal negative+(base be-verb+cont)*	*pr+sgctcn+(dadj+sgctcn) (tphr)*
They	**won't+be+going**	**on+holiday+(this+year).**

Note: *If my abbreviations confuse you at first, refer back to the previous page; don't worry, you'll learn them in no time. You might want to use these grammatical abbreviations in your own classes.*

Example:

Provide something like this on the board or by OHP.

1st person	prc	uctcn	tphr

The students can then interpret this into actual language;like this.

I	am playing am making am drinking etc.	football cheese water etc.	today. this week. at the moment. etc.

The basic Passive sentence consists of		
the complement (object)	**the verb**	**and the subject**
The objects consist of items that do not perform the action – they are affected upon. However, the object must be able to be affected upon. So a sentence such as, 'I live in Auckland' cannot become 'Auckland is lived in by me'.	The verb consists of various aspects of the be-verb followed by the past (3rd) participle; either regular (~ed verbs), irregular (different [new] verbs) or verbs that don't change at all! Or revert to the base verb – it can all be so confusing! Present simple = is/am/are+3rd/ past participle Past simple = was/ were+3rd/past participle Present continuous = is/am/are+being+3rd/ past participle Past continuous = was/ were+being+3rd/past participle Present perfect = have/has been+3rd/ past participle Past perfect = had been+3rd/past participle Modal = modal+be-verb+3rd/past participle Semi-modal = semi-modal+be-verb+3rd/past participle *Beyond this point it isn't common usage.* Present perfect continuous = have/has been being+3rd/past participle Past perfect continuous = had been being+3rd/past participle	The subject consists of the 'actor' or 'do-er' of the action but is often not mentioned in these types of sentences. The subject can also be a time or a place. The preposition '**by**' often precedes the subject.

Passive sentences.

Italics: actual grammar (parts of speech).
Bold: actual words.
See page 18 for explanation of parts of speech

complement	be-verb+3rd/Past participle	Subject
cnadj+plctcn	*plprs (be-verb)+3rd/past participle*	*pr+uctcn*
Car bodies	**are made**	**with+fibreglass.**
dart+PN	*pts (be-verb)+3rd/past participle*	*pr+PN.*
The+Mona Lisa	**was+painted**	**by+Leonardo de Vinci**
sgpsn+sgctcn	*pts (be-verb)+3rd/past participle*	*pr+PN (country).*
My+watch	**was+made**	**in+Switzerland.**
dart+sgctcn	*prc+3rd/past participle*	*(pr+dart+sgctcn) (tphr).*
The+house	**is being+built**	**(at+the+moment).**
	Past continuous sentences need two sentences as in the active form using 'when' or 'while'.	
dart+sgctcn	*pp+3rd/past participle*	*pr+(adj+plctcn) (tphr).*
The+violin	**has been+played**	**for+(many years).**
dart+uctcn	*ptp+3rd/past participle*	*past (tphr)*
The+grass	**had been+mown**	**three weeks ago.**
plpn	*m+be+3rd/past participle*	*pr+dart+sgctcn+pr+sgctcn.*
They	**could+be+taken**	**to+the+cinema+by+bus.**
plpn	*sm+be+3rd/past participle*	*pr+dart+sgctcn+pr+sgctcn.*
They	**want to+be+taken**	**to+the+cinema+by+bus.**

4/2371853

Imperative sentences: Base verb+object+complement.		
base verb	**proper nouns/object pronouns**	**complement**
Do Lend	Peter me	a favour. your pen.
Get Put Sit	them	out! on the table. down!

Exclamatory sentences with: What+(article)*+adjective+c.noun (!)+(subject+verb)!**					
What	**article***	**adjective**	**common noun**	**(subject**	**verb)!**
What	a	beautiful	house (!)	(he	has!)
What		beautiful	flowers (!)	(they	received!)

And: How+adjective+(subject+verb*)! How+adverb+(subject+verb*)!		
How	**adjective/adverb**	**(subject+verb)****
How How	lovely! slowly	(it looks) it moves!
*articles are not necessary with plurals or uncountables. **the subject and verb combination is also not always necessary.		

Interrogative sentences: See pages 55 & 165 for a more detailed coverage.	
Here are examples of CLOSED, OPEN and TAG questions:	
CLOSED	Are you learning English? Is he a teacher? Can you come to class tomorrow? Did he pass the exam?
OPEN	What are you learning? Who is your teacher? Where do you come from? When will they arrive?
TAG	You are learning English, aren't you? She is your teacher, isn't she? They can sing, can't they?

THERE/IT

There *is used when we want to show that something exists in a* **specific** *place; it is mainly used with* **be- verbs,** *and* **have, has** *and* **had** *in perfect sentences. The* **singular** *verbs are used with singular common or uncountable nouns. Look at these sentences.*

There is a table in the room.
There is water in the glass.
There has been an accident in this street.

The plural verb is used with plural common nouns. Look at these sentences.

There are boys in the park.
There are five chairs in the room.
There have been several accidents in this street.

It, *besides being a pronoun, is also used to indicate a climatic or weather condition, a state or date and time. Look at these sentences.*

It is raining.
It is a hot today.
Put on a jacket, it's cold outside.
It is six o'clock.
It is Monday today.

Quite a few languages simply say;

Table is in the room.
Water is in the glass.
Today is hot. Outside is cold, etc.,

so it is necessary to point out this usage of **there** and **it.**

PART 2
Parts of speech

PARTS OF SPEECH

adjectives	adverbs	articles	auxiliary verbs	conjunctions	modals	semi-modals
base, comparative, superlative, demonstrative*, ~ed, gerund, 3rd/ past participle, suffix, adjective order, no.	comment, manner, frequency, degree, time, place, with present perfect, not.	indefinite, definite.	be-verbs, simple verbs, perfect verbs.	similar, contrast, conditional, purpose, reason, result, time phrases. how.	can, could, will, would, may, might, (shall), should, must.	able to, dare to, going to, have to, etc.

nouns	prefixes	suffixes	prepositions	pronouns	punctuation	question words
abstract, common (concrete), proper, gerunds.	dis~, un~, il~, im~, etc.	~al, ~ive, ~ment, ~ion, etc.	position, time, duration, direction, sequence, etc.	subject, object, demonstrative*, possessive, possessive adjective, reflexive, relative.	comma, colon, semi-colon, full-stop etc.	What, Which, Who, Whom, Where, When, Whose, Why, How.

*Demonstratives** act both as **adjectives**; 'This book ..' and **pronouns**; '**This** is a book.' There are also other uses.

DETERMINERS: are words you might see before common nouns, the most common of which are the articles; then there are possessive adjectives, possessive proper nouns, demonstrative adjectives, etc. **Most English sentences need one of these.**

Tenses

aspects*	function
Present simple	indicates facts, unchanging conditions, routines, etc.
Past simple	indicates events or conditions (states) in the past at a definite time.
Present continuous	indicates events in the present and changing conditions.
Past continuous	indicates 'enveloping' events in the past.
Present perfect	indicates events in one's life, has no indication of specific time.
Past perfect	indicates an event preceding a past event.
Present perfect continuous	indicates an event started in the past and may continue, possibly, into the future.
Past perfect continuous	has almost the same connotation as the past continuous.
Auxiliary verbs	serve several functions in combination with other verbs. **See page 34 & 62**
Modals**	modify the function of main verbs.
Semi-modals**	modify the function of main verbs.
Future**	English doesn't really have a future form; **future time** converts a sentence into the future.

Tenses and Aspects

*Simply put; **tense** denotes the three universal sense of time; **past, present** and **future** while **aspect** denotes a further split within the tenses. So the **past** can be expressed in these (**aspect**) ways; I **visited** Spain last year; I **was living** in Spain when ...; I **have lived** in Spain, and so on. The **present** can be expressed in these ways; I **live** in New Zealand; I **am living** in New Zealand and the **future** with the **present simple**; I **leave tomorrow** at 8.00 am and the **present continuous**; I'm **leaving tomorrow** at 8.00 am. Future intentions can also be converted to the concrete future by adding the future time; I **will** see you **tomorrow**; I'm **going to** see you **tomorrow**.

The modal **will or the semi-modal **be-verb+going to** put before the present simple base verb can indicate a possible action in the future; I **will see** him; I'm **going to see** him; they become more concrete when a future time is added.

When the modal **will** or the semi-modal **be-verb+going to** is put before the present continuous, it suggests that some action will be in progress at a future time. I **will be living** in Spain next year; I'm **going to be living** in Spain next year.

When the modal **will** is put before the present perfect, the sentence suggests a definite anticipation; I **will have seen** five films by the end of the month. By stating this I feel very sure that I will accomplish it. He **will have left** by 10.00 pm tonight. I feel very sure that after 10.00 pm he will no longer be here.

Other modals and semi–modals may also be used, but they might suggest other connotations.

See Modals on page 40 and 91 and Semi-modals on page 44 and 93.

POSITION AND FUNCTION
of the Parts of speech

Part of Speech	Types	Position & Function	Form	Example
Adjectives	Base	are placed before common nouns. They help to identify and differentiate people and things.	The word does not change. They cannot be made into plural words.	big houses **NOT** bigs houses.
	Comparative	are placed between **2** items, persons, groups, etc. They show the difference between things and compares them.	usually take an ~er suffix followed by **than**. Some long adjectives follow the word **more**.	This house is bigger than that house. This book is **more** interesting **than** that book.
	Superlative	are placed before common nouns or after auxiliary verbs. They show the uniqueness of an object.	take an ~est suffix; they follow the word **the**. The long adjectives remain unchanged, but follow the words **the most.**	This house is **the biggest**. This is **the biggest** house. This is **the most** expensive house on the street.
	Demonstrative	are placed before common nouns and adjectives which are before common nouns. **This** and **these** indicate nearness in time and place. They are tactile words. **That** and **those** indicate distance in time and place. They are often accompanied by finger-pointing.	there are only four; **this, that, these, those.**	**This** book is mine. **Those** books are mine.
	~ed	take the same position as base adjectives. They show a feeling, mood or state.	follow the same rules as regular adjectives.	Billy the Kid was a wanted man. He looks very tired.
	~ing (gerund)	take the same position as base adjectives. They show opinions or use.	follow the same rules as regular adjectives.	It was an interesting film. Where's the nearest shopping centre?
	past simple & 3rd/ past participle irregular verb	take the same position as base adjectives. They show a state or condition.	follow the same rules as regular adjectives.	The shelf was full of **filled** bottles. The **broken** glass was removed from the street.
	suffix	are added to the end of nouns; similar to ~ed and ~ing.	~(t)ic, ~ful, ~ive, etc.	It was a dramatic moment. It was a beautiful movie.

Parts of speech	Types	Position and Function	Form	Example
Adverbs	comment	are generally put at the beginning of the sentence. They express an opinion or feeling.	generally take the suffix ~ly.	**Personally**, I didn't enjoy the film.
	manner	are usually put before or after the main verb or at the end of the sentence. They explain how an action was done.	generally take the suffix ~ly.	He (**carefully**) climbed (**carefully**) up the tree. He climbed up the tree **carefully**.
	frequency	are usually put before the main verb and between be-verb and adjective. They show how often an action occurs.	The more common words are: **always, frequently, often, sometimes, usually, seldom, rarely, hardly ever, never, ~n't ever.** These also include words such as **once, twice,** etc.	Peter **always** comes late to class. I am **often** asked this question. John is **often** late. I visit the zoo **twice a year**.
	degree	are put before an adverb or adjective. They raise or lower the quality of the adverb or adjective.	The more common words are: **very, quite, too, rather, pretty, so, such a,** etc.	She does her homework **very** carefully. The meal was **pretty** expensive.
	time	can be put at the beginning of the sentence or at the end. They show the time an action occurs. They are usually phrases.	Dates, years, clock time; words like **next, ago, last, yesterday, tomorrow,** etc.	**Next year,** I'm going home. I'm going home **next year**. They met at **6.00 pm**.
	place	are usually put at the end of the sentence. They show where an action occurs. They are usually phrases.	Any location: **in the cinema, at school, on the street,** etc.	I'll meet you **at the café**. They lived **in a small town**. They are sitting over **there**.
	also	is usually put between subject and main verb or at the end of the sentence. It shows an addition, but can be ambiguous.		She **also** speaks French. She speaks French **also**.

after/before	Usually after first object. **See Conjunctions on page 38 and page 88.**		I do my homework **after/before** dinner.
present perfect (adverb)	There are six common adverbs which go into different positions in the sentence. They modify the verbs in different ways.	subject aux-verb]**adverb**[3rd/past participle completion. subject]**adverb**[neg aux-verb 3rd/past participle completion. subject neg sentence] **adverb**. closed question]**adverb**? subject aux-verb]**adverb**[3rd/past participle completion. subject neg. aux-verb]**adverb**[3rd/past participle completion.	I have **already** eaten. I have **just** eaten. He **still** hasn't come. I haven't seen him **yet**. Have you seen him **yet**? I have **never** seen that boy. I haven't **ever** seen that boy.

Parts of Speech	Types	Position & Function	Form	Example
Articles	indefinite definite		a, an, the (/ðə/, /ði:/)	
	a (/əi/)	is put before a first reference of a common, singular noun. Not used with plural words and uncountable nouns; however, it can be used with pronouns or proper nouns. It shows that what is being referred to is one of many.	Pronounced 'uh' (/ə/)	I have a book. Is it a he or a she? There is a Mr Smith to see you. NOT I have a books. I have a water.
	an (/æn/)	has the same function as 'a' but is put before common, singular nouns that starts with a vowel SOUND.*	Pronounced /æn/ and usually joined to the next word when spoken.	I have /æn/ umbrella (/ə/ Numbrella).
	'the'	unlike the indefinite article the definite article has no other written form, but it has two different pronunciations as shown below. It shows that what is being referred to, singular, plural common nouns or uncountables have a certain specificity. There are approximately 26 different uses.		I bought a book yesterday. The book I bought was quite expensive. The capital of New Zealand is Wellington.
	'thuh' (/ðə/)	is spoken before common nouns that begin with consonant SOUNDS		The (/ðə/) book is quite expensive.
	'thee' (/ði:/)	is spoken before common nouns that begin with vowel SOUNDS	Usually joined to the next word when spoken.	The (/ði:/elephant) elephant is a large animal.

Vowel SOUND: the idea that an and the (/ði:/) precede words beginning with a, e, i, o, u should be discouraged.

Part of Speech	Types	Position & Function	Form	Example
(Primary) Auxiliary verbs be-verbs		are used both as main verb and as auxiliary verb to show a continuing action. When they are used in the present simple form, they show the existence of something; when used in the past simple they signify a condition in the past that may no longer exist. They are used to form questions and negative sentences.		See below.
	am	is used only with the pronoun 'I' (first person) 'am not' is not abbreviated into 'amn't'.	1st person subject **am** (complement). subject **am** base-verb+ing completion.	I **am** a teacher. I **am** teaching English.
	is	is used with 'He', 'She', 'It', (third person/ singular), singular common nouns, uncountable nouns and proper nouns.	3rd person subject **is** complement. **Is** subject base-verb+ing complement?	The teacher **isn't** here today. **Is** Peter taking a holiday?
	are	is used with 'You', 'They', 'We' and plural common nouns. It is not used with proper nouns and uncountable nouns unless they are in the plural form.	2nd person subject **are** complement. subject **are** negative complement. subject **are** base-verb+ing completion.	You **are** late today. The students **aren't** late today. The students **are** doing an exam. The Smiths **are** coming.
	was	is the past form of 'am', and 'is'. When it is used in the continuous form, it usually consists of TWO sentences joined by the conjunctions 'when' or 'while'.	1st & 3rd person subject **was** complement. **Was** subject base-verb+ing complement?	I **was** a teacher in my country. **Was** she dancing *when* she fell?
	were	is the past form of 'are'. When it is used in the continuous form, it serves the same function as 'was'.	(plural) subject **were** completion. Same as 'was' continuous.	They **were** teachers in their country.

(Dummy) Auxiliary verbs Simple verbs	are the 'invisible' auxiliary verbs as they do not exist in the original, affirmative sentence. As main verb, they are put between subject and completion; in closed questions they are put at the beginning of the sentence; in open questions they are put after the question word with the main verb being a base verb. In negative sentences they are put before the base verb combined with 'not' (n't). They may also be used to emphasize the main verb, in which case they are put before the main (base) verb. They show habitual behaviour or the lack of one in the case of a negative sentence.		I **shop** on Saturdays. (base sentence). NOTE: the auxiliary verb is absent/'invisible'. I **do** like you.
do	is used with first & second persons and plural pronouns & common nouns.	1st/2nd person or plural subject **do** completion.	I **do** my housework on Saturdays. **Do** they **do** their shopping on Saturdays?
does	is used with third person, proper nouns and singular common nouns.	3rd person/proper nouns/singular common nouns subject **does** complement.	He **does** his shopping on Saturdays. Mary **doesn't do** her shopping on Saturdays. What **does** the cook **do** on Saturdays?
did	is used with all forms of subjects. It shows an action in the past which is no longer active.	1st, 2nd, 3rd person/ singular and plural nouns **did** completion.	I **did** my shopping last week. You **did** your shopping last week. They **didn't do** their shopping last week.

	do/does/did		Used with the above subjects; placed before the main (base) verbs	I do like to eat fish. Mary **does** know how to drive. I **did** tell you about the party.
(Primary) **Auxiliary verbs** **Perfect verbs**		can be used to emphasize.		

when used as main verbs they are put between subject and completion; when used as auxiliary verbs they are put before the 3rd/past participle; in closed questions they are put at the beginning of the sentence and in open questions they are put after the question word with the main verb being a 3rd/past participle.

When used as negative they are put before the 3rd/past participle verb with 'not' (n't).

As main verb they generally show possession, but have other meanings as well.

As main verbs they can, in some instances, be made into the negative form. **See page 84.**

have	is used with first & second person and plural pronouns & common nouns.	1st/2nd person/plurals/ **have** complement. subject **have** 3rd/ past participle complement. **Have** subject 3rd/past participle completion? subject **have** neg 3rd/ past participle complement adverb.	I/You/The boys **have** breakfast at 8.00am. I **have** had breakfast. **Have** you bought the house? The children **haven't** come home yet.
has	is used with third person, proper nouns & singular & uncountable common nouns.	3rd person/proper nouns/singular/ uncountable nouns **has** 3rd/past participle completion. Q word **has** subject 3rd participle completion?	He/Peter/The boy **has** breakfast at 8.00am. The coffee **hasn't got** milk in it. He/The boy **has** played tennis before. What **has** Mary baked?
had	is used with all forms of subject. In the past perfect form it suggests an intervening period. Not in common use in closed questions.	1st/2nd/3rd/common nouns/plurals/ uncountables **had** completion.	I/He/The boy/ **had** a dog when I /he/the boy was a child. You/They/The boys **had** a dog when you/ they/ the boys were children. Had he bought the car?

Part of Speech	Types	Position & Function	Form	Example
Conjunctions		are generally put between two complete sentences or 2 nouns, verbs, adjectives, etc; depending on what is being combined or contrasted, etc.	sentence **conj** sentence. noun **conj** noun, etc.	I play sport **and** I play the piano. Peter **and** I sing **and** dance.
	similar	As above.	idea **and** idea; adjective **and** adjective, etc.	She has a dog **and** she likes visiting the zoo. She was tall **and** blonde.
	contrast	As above.	positive idea **but** negative idea. negative idea **but** positive idea. one, not the other.	Mary passed **but** Peter failed. Peter didn't come **but** Mary did. Mary, **but** not Peter ...
	conditional	consist of TWO sentences joined by the conjunction **if, unless,** etc. They indicate a situation which might make a desire possible or not.	**See page 144**	
	reason	usually put between two sentences and explain why something was or was not done.	action sentence **because** reason sentence.	I went to the shop **because** I wanted to buy an ice cream.
	purpose	similar to **reason** but with the use of **to.**	action **to** reason/purpose.	I went to the shop **to** buy an ice cream.
	result	put between two complete sentences and show cause and effect.	cause **so** effect.	He was tired **so** he went to bed early.

time clauses	consist of two sentences; a past simple and a past continuous and the conjunctions used are **when** and **while**; **When** precedes the past simple sentence and **while** precedes the past continuous sentence.	past continuous sentence **when** past simple sentence. past simple sentence **while** past continuous sentence.	He was coming to school **when** he saw the accident. He saw the accident **while** he was coming to school.
	As can stand in for **while** in some cases.	**As** past continuous sentence, past continuous sentence.	**As** they were arriving, we were leaving.
how	is an adverb and a conjunction and a question word.	sentence **how** sentence. sentence	
	It shows the way or method something is done; usually followed by **to**.	**how to** sentence.	I'll show you **how** I make this. I'll show you **how to** make this.
	It is also a question word. **See page 174.**	**How** question sentence?	**How** are you today?

There are many more: see CONJUNCTIONS on page 88.

Part of Speech	Types	Position & Function	Form	Example
Modals	There is a tendency to put modals in the same basket with auxiliary verbs. They are often referred to as auxiliary **VERBS**, which is confusing because they cannot be used as main verbs the way auxiliary verbs can; nor do they have true past forms. They can be used in future sentences.	are put before base verbs or followed by base verbs; whatever you choose. can — be could — play will — have would — see may — go might — buy shall — take should — eat must — watch etc They change the meaning of the verb to a slight degree. They serve several functions. They are used in conditional sentences, of which the third conditional is in the past and is true; in an opposite sense. **For Conditional use of Modals see pages 91 and 144.**		

	Usage	Structure	Example
can	indicates an ability;	subject **can** base-verb complement.	That girl **can** play football well.
	in question form queries an ability;	**Can** subject base-verb completion?	**Can** he sing?
	a possibility;	subject **can** base-verb object complement.	Be careful; it **can** break.
	permission or request. (colloquial use)	**Can** (nouns or pronouns) base-verb completion?	**Can** I borrow your pen?
could	indicates a past ability; (possible present inability)	subject **could** base-verb completion. (past time phrase).	I **could** sing (beautifully) before I was 13.
	indicates a polite request;	**Could** subject base-verb completion?	**Could** I borrow your pen?
	a suggestion;	**Could** subject base-verb completion? subject **could** suggestion.	You **could** take a taxi.
	it is used with **wish(es)**;	subject *wish(es)* subject **could** base-verb completion.	I wish I **could** buy that car.
	it can be used to speculate;	subject **could** base-verb completion? speaker (past simple) subject **could** base-verb completion.	She **could** be a doctor?
	it is used in reported speech.		He said he **could** see me tomorrow.
will	indicates a strong desire to do something;	Subject **will** base-verb completion.	I **will** buy a car someday.
	it indicates a sudden decision or unplanned decision; unexpected situation;		"No fish! OK, I **will** have the steak."
	indicates a prediction; often preceded by phrases that show uncertainty.	Subject **will** base-verb completion.	It **will** rain tomorrow. Maybe it'll rain tomorrow.

	Usage	Structure	Examples
would	indicates repeated action in the past; (infers the behaviour is discontinued) it indicates a polite offer with **like** or **like to** base-verb; it is used with **wish(es)**; it is used in reported speech.	subject **would** base- verb completion. conjunction (when) subject past verb completion. **Would** subject *like/like to* completion? subject *wish(es)* subject **would** base-verb completion. speaker subject **would** base-verb completion.	I **would** run 20kms a day, when I played sport. (Maybe, I don't now). **Would** you **like** an ice cream? / **Would** you **like to** have an ice cream? He wishes you **wouldn't** talk so loudly. He said he **would** buy that house.
may	indicates permission; indicates a possibility; a wish; not generally used in tag questions; combined with **be** it shows uncertainty	subject **may** base-verb completion. (and also in question forms) subject **may** base-verb completion. **May** subject present simple completion. **Maybe** subject predition.	You **may** leave the room. **May** he come in? He **may** be in the room. It **may** rain tomorrow. **May** you have a happy life. He **may come, mayn't he?** **Maybe** it will rain.
might	indicates a possibility; (but unlikely) indicates a suggestion with 'I'; (not common) not generally used in tag questions, but it's possible …	subject **might** base-verb completion. **Might** 1st person subject object/person complement.	It's a lovely day, but it **might** rain. **Might** I suggest you pay in cash. It **might** rain, **mightn't** it? (hhmm?)

shall	its current use is always in the question form; It indicates an offer with 'I';	**Shall** I base-verb completion? **Shall** we base-verb completion?	**Shall** I pass you the sugar? **Shall** we go to the cinema tonight?
	It indicates a suggestion with 'we'. It is not normally used with any other subjects; when implying doubt of a future outcome, we use ... and the negative, believe it or not, is ... and has an archaic imperative use.		**We shall see. shan't** You **shall** bow before the king.
should	indicates a suggestion; or advisability; it can be used to show anticipation; it is used in reported speech.	subject **should** base- verb completion. same as above, depending on its seriousness. subject **should** base- verb completion. speaker subject **should** base-verb completion.	You **should** see that film. You **should** see a doctor. They **should** arrive soon. He said you **should** see a doctor.
must	indicates a strong obligation or necessity; rule or law; it indicates one's own obligation to one's self; it is used to show a very sure guess; it has no 'past' form. **Had to** is used as the past form of must.	subject **must** base- verb completion. subject **must** base verb completion. subject **had to** base verb completion.	You **must** obey the law. I **must** study hard; I want to pass the exam. That **must** be the railway station. They **had to** do a test yesterday.

Part of Speech	Types	Position & Function	Form	Example
Semi-modals		take the same position as the modals in the sentence but they are comprised of a verb and the preposition 'to'. They are also followed by the base verb. They can be used in most of their tense forms and in conjunction with modals.		
	be-verb able to	indicates having the skill to do something; in some ways similar to 'can' but suggests a little more effort.	subject be-verb **able to** base-verb complement.	They **are able to** use the computer well.
	dare to	indicates having the courage, taking a risk, being brave; challenge someone to something.	subject **dare to** base- verb complement.	He **dares to** challenge his teachers. Will you **dare to** touch that tiger? She **dared to** fight him.
	be-verb going to	indicates having a strong intention to do something.	subject **be-verb going to** base-verb complement.	She's **going to** leave her boyfriend. **Are** you **going to** buy that book?
	have to	indicates having a strong obligation to do something which one might not want to do. The negative form removes any obligation and suggests a choice.	subject **have to** base- verb object. n't **have to**	I don't want to, but I **have to** leave now. You **don't have to** go now; you can go later if you wish.
	hope to	indicates having a wish or desire.	same as above.	She **hopes to** complete her studies this year. What do you **hope to** do next year?
	like to	indicates enjoying an activity.	same as above.	They **like to** play in the rain. Do you **like to** eat fish?

need to	indicates having a necessity to do something; the negative form removes any obligation and suggests a choice, very much like **don't have to**. Not commonly used in the continuous form.	same as above.	I **need to** put more petrol in the car. Do you **need to** talk to me right now? You **don't need to** come if you don't want to. I ~~am needing to~~ buy a book.
ought to	is the equivalent of **should**; indicates a suggestion; indicates advisibility; it is used in reported speech.	subject **ought to** base- verb complement. same as above, depending on its seriousness. speaker subject **ought to** base-verb complement.	You **ought to** see that film. You **ought to** see a doctor. He said you **ought to** see a doctor.
plan to	indicates thinking about doing something.	same as above.	She **plans to** go abroad next year. Are you **planning to** go anywhere for the holidays? What are you **planning to** do?
be-verb supposed to	indicates an intended action or plan.	subject be-verb **supposed to** complement.	He **was supposed to** be here by 5.00 pm. Who **is supposed to** bring the cake?
(be-verb) used to	indicates a discontinued habit, custom, or behaviour in the past; can be individual or communal. the be-verb gives it a time phase; in this form the main verb is a gerund (noun).	subject **used to** base- verb complement. subject be-verb **used to** gerund complement.	I **used to** play a lot of sport when I was at school. The Smiths **used to** live in Australia. I **am used to** eating with my fingers.

		subject **want to** base- verb complement.	He **wants to** do well in the exam. The children **want to** go to the zoo this Saturday.
want to	indicates having a personal desire		
would like to	is almost like 'want to', with perhaps more pleasure.	same as above.	I **would like to** take you out to dinner. **Would** you **like to** come with me? I **wouldn't like to** be in his shoes!

Part of Speech	Types	Position & Function	Form	Example
Nouns		Abstract nouns may or may not follow adjectival pronouns.		**Love** makes the world go round. My **love** for you is eternal.
		Singular concrete nouns usually follow articles, possessive or demonstrative pronouns, adjectives and also the possessive **'s**.		A **book** My **book**. **This** book. This interesting **book.** Peter's **book.** A **book** is for reading. I am reading a **book.**
		Generally give names to things. They can be subjects or objects of sentences.		
	abstract	are always in the singular; they are the names of things that are not generally tangible; you can feel them, sense them but you can't put them in your pocket.		Everyone seeks **happiness.** **Failure** is hard to accept. They sought **warmth** under the bridge.
	concrete (common)	are the names of things that are tangible; they can be identified; many objects share the same name though they may look different.		Put the **chair** near the **table.** These **boys** want to play with those **girls.**
	proper	are the specific names of people, cities, countries, book, films, etc; they are usually singular; the first letter is always capital.		**Peter** lives in **London**, **England.** I saw **Life of Pi** at the **Lido** two weeks ago.
	gerunds	are base verbs ending with ~**ing** but behave as nouns or adjectives; in most cases also follow prepositions and certain verbs such as **enjoy.** **See page 152.**	**relaxing, swimming, shopping, eating,** etc.	**Walking** is good exercise. I go **swimming** as often as I can. I enjoy **reading.**

Part of Speech	Types	Position & Function	Form	Example
Prefixes		are small words or part of words that are attached to the beginning of other words which then undergo a change in meaning, usually for the opposite. Some prepositions and adverbs may also be used as prefixes.	**im-, in-, non-**, etc.	**im**possible; **anti**-hero, etc.
Suffixes		are attached to the end of words. They, unlike prefixes, affect the function of the word. Adjectives become abstract nouns, nouns become adjectives, etc. The original word might experience some changes in spelling. They don't change the meaning of the original word.	-ity, -al, -ly, etc.	happi**ness**; sensib**le**, etc.

Part of Speech	Types	Position & Function	Form	Example
Prepositions		are put after the main verb or the first object of the sentence. They connect the verb to the object of the sentence. Each preposition performs different functions. They are usually followed by nouns or gerunds; however, 'to' is not commonly followed by gerunds but it has its exceptions. Some adverbs also take the same position as prepositions. They can change the meaning of the verb, then it becomes a **Phrasal verb.** **See page 162.**	subject verb preposition 1st object preposition 2nd object.	I come to school **by** bus. I come to school **at** 8.00 am.

Part of Speech	Types	Position & Function	Form	Example
Pronouns	There are several types of pronouns.			
	subject	are in the subject space of the sentence. They refer to something or someone already mentioned. At the beginning of the sentence they take capital letters. However, 'I' is always in capital no matter where in the sentence!	I, You, He, She, They, We, It.	I am a teacher. He plays football. It is lovely. Does she play tennis? Do you have the time? Do I look good in this dress?
	object	are in the completion space of the sentences. They refer to something or someone already mentioned in subject or completion space of the sentence. They hardly ever take capital letters. With the exception of you and it the other subject pronouns change when used in the object position.	me, you, him, her, them, us, it.	He gave me a book. I told you the truth. Look at it.
	demonstrative	can be put before a common noun (adjective) or can stand on their own (pronoun). They have both singular and plural forms. This/these indicate nearness in place and time, could also indicate touching; that/those indicate distance in place and time and is often accompanied by pointing.	this, these; that, those.	This is a book. Those books are mine. I'm playing football this weekend. What is that over there?
	possessive adjectives	are put before common nouns. If there are adjectives before the common noun then they are put before the adjective(s). They indicate ownership of the object.	my, your, his, her, their, our its.	This is my book. Where is your red book?

possessive pronouns	are used both as subject and object of a sentence. They are not followed by common nouns. They show ownership of object(s) already indicated.	mine, yours, his, hers, theirs, ours, its.	This is **mine**. Where is **yours**? **Mine** is over there.
reflexive	can be put immediately after a subject noun/pronoun/proper noun or in the object position. When used after the subject it indicates an emphasis; when used as the object of the sentence, it indicates that the subject and the object are one and the same.	myself, yourself, yourselves, himself, herself, themselves, ourselves, itself.	I **myself** saw the accident. I gave **myself** a present. Peter **himself** told me. Peter told **himself** he had to change.
relatives	are usually put immediately after the subject or object regarding which something needs to be said. They are, in fact, the same as question words, with the exception of **what** which becomes **that**. Having said that; there are instances where **what** too can be a relative pronoun. **See page 175.**	who, that, which, who(m), whose, when, where, why.	The man **who** brought this book is a teacher. My teacher, **who** comes from Iran, brought this book. I gave the book to a man **who(m)** I met on the street. I don't like **what** you just said.

There are other types of pronouns as well; such as someone, everyone, much, each, etc.

Part of Speech	Types	Position & Function	Form	Example
Punctuation		These help the reader to get a better understanding of the text; particularly when reading the text aloud.		
	full stop, point, period	is used to indicate the end of a sentence or an idea, an abbreviation, a decimal point, in time and dates.	.	I am happy. The U.S.A. 0.05. 8.30am. 30.12.1940.
	comma	Here are some of the uses of the comma: 1. Lists (series). 2. Adjectives. 3. Separate conjunctival sentences. 4. Informative relative clauses or phrases. 5. Adverbs. 6. Numbers. 7. Before conjunctions in lengthy sentences.	,	I visited Spain, France, Germany, etc. He was a tall, dark, mysterious man. If I see him, I'll tell him. Peter, who teaches English, is also an actor. John, surprisingly, is a very good tennis player. 3,200. 300,200. 3,300,200 I decided to stay home and read, but Mary chose to go to the cinema with Bob.

colon	:	is used before an explanation or amplification; in dialogues (scripts); before lists; in subtitles.	We decided not to drive to the coast: the weather had changed for the worse. John: Do you love me? Mary: Don't be daft! Here are some of the things we can buy: sugar, cheese, bread, milk, etc. Anthropology: The study of mankind.
semi-colon	;	is used instead of a full stop, especially with closely related sentences; can separate a series of actions. This one is tricky – it seems to be losing it proper use.	It's a lovely morning; hope it stays that way. First, I'm thinking of going to the supermarket; then perhaps, I'll go to the gym; or maybe, I'll stop off at a cafe and have a coffee.
dash	–	can be used in the same way as colons, semi-colons, or brackets, with space before and after the dash.	I'm interested – if the price is right.
hyphen	-	is used to join some prefixes to the main word, creates compound words; two word adjectives; phrases as adjectives. It is shorter than the dash and has no spaces.	co-author. box-office. blue-eyed. shoot-to-kill policy.
question mark	?	is put at the end of a sentence to indicate a question or query, confusion, uncertainty.	Are you happy? You're not coming? $200?
exclamation mark	!	indicates a shout, or emphasis, wonderment.	Hey! Well done!

Name	Symbol	Description	What!?
interrobang	!?/?!	is a combination of an exclamation mark and a question mark to indicate surprise, astonishment, etc.	What!?
brackets or parenthesis	( )	are used to indicate an aside or extra information, dates, explanations, truncated relative clauses, etc.	He arrived on time (just). Herman Hesse (1877 – 1962). He was absent (ill). John (a teacher) lives in Spain.
quotation marks, inverted commas, quote marks	"—" '—'	are used to indicate direct speech or text taken from another source; they can be "double" or 'single' commas. The north American usage differs from the British usage. But there is considerable overlap. Simply – use double commas for dialogue within a text (narrative) and single commas from extracts from other sources, or to differentiate words from the main text of your writing. The double commas can also be used to indicate irony in written text and by folding and unfolding the first two fingers of both hands in the air.	She said, "I love you." He said, "The word 'row' can be a verb or noun depending on how you pronounce it; or the context within which it is used." His concept of "justice", as he sees it, is a bit skewed. "Yes, I think he's a very "clever" man." (Wriggle your fingers!)
forward slash	/	is used to separate date/month/year; in place of 'or', avoiding a choice; showing fractions.	30/12/1940. male/female. ¾.
apostrophe	'	indicates omitted letters or words and is a sign of possession.	can't Peter's car

Part of Speech	Types	Position & Function	Form	Example
Question words		are always placed at the beginning of the sentence and is usually followed by an auxiliary verb or modal, depending on the tense used. **What**, **Which** and **Whose** can also be followed by nouns. **How** can be followed by adjectives or adverbs.		See below.
	What	The answer it usually seeks is related to things or enquires after some action or activity.	**What** verb subject completion? **What** aux subject ~ing+verb completion? **What** modal subject base+verb completion?	**What** is this? **What** have you done today? **What** is he doing at work today? **What** can we do today?
		A noun can be put after 'What'; in which case the enquiry is regarding the noun.		**What** *book* do you want to buy?
	Which	has the same question structure as **What**. Often used to signify a choice from a limited stock. The phrase '**of the**' is often used after '**Which**' but not after '**What**'. It is quite often followed by a noun.	See above.	**Which** is your book? **Which** are the cheapest shoes? **Which** *of the shoes* are the cheapest? **Which** *shoes* are the cheapest?
	Who	The answer to 'Who' is usually the subject of the sentence but it can also be the object of the sentence; to form a 'Who' question, put it before the verb or auxiliary/modal verb; when used with a preposition, the preposition is put at the end of the sentence.	**Who** verb subject/ object completion? **Who** aux subject ~ing+verb completion? **Who** modal subject base+verb completion?	**Who** is that man? **Who** gave you a book? **Who** were you talking *to*? **Who** have you seen today? **Who** can I give this book *to*?

Whom	is a more formal version of 'Who'; when used with a preposition, the preposition is usually put before 'whom'. It refers to the 'object' person. Some people consider ending a sentence with a preposition inelegant!	See above.	**Whom** shall I see? *To* **whom** is this important? *From* **whom** did you get this book? **Whom** is this important *to?* **Whom** did you get this book *from?*
Where	is used to find a person(s) or thing(s) or the place(s) or location(s) of something.	See above.	**Where** can I find good shoes? **Where** is Peter?
When	is generally answered with a '**broad**' time as opposed to **What time**; which requires a more exact answer.	See above.	**When** can you leave? **When** do you do the shopping?
Whose	is usually followed by a common noun regarding which an owner needs to be identified; when the item is obvious, it may not be mentioned. Queries ownership.	See above.	**Whose** *book* is this? **Whose** *shoes* are you wearing? **Whose** are these?
Why	is asking for the reason for something to have occurred. The answer often includes the conjunction **because.** Used in the negative form it might be enquiring after an expected action not being fulfilled or offering a suggestion.	See above.	**Why** is the Ganges River so polluted? **Why** *isn't* Peter here? **Why** *don't* you see a doctor?
How	usually asks about the manner or method something is performed, it can be followed by an adjective or adverb.	**See page 174.**	**How** fast do dolphins swim? **How** do you come to school?

TENSES

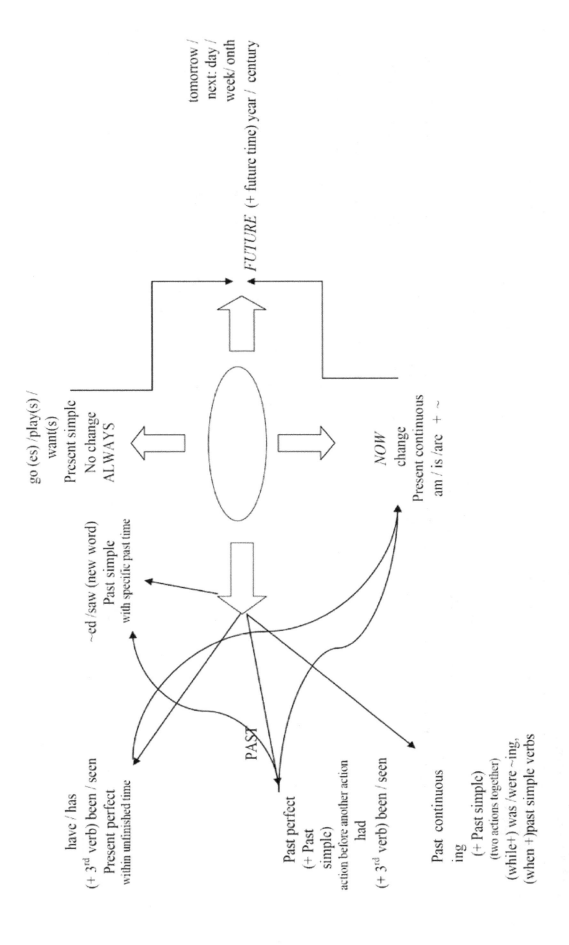

FUTURE (+ future time) year / century

tomorrow /
next: day /
week/ onth

go (es) /play(s) /
want(s)
Present simple
No change
ALWAYS

NOW
change
Present continuous
am / is /are + ~

have / has
(+ 3rd verb) been / seen
Present perfect
within unfinished time

~ed /saw (new word)
Past simple
with specific past time

PAST

Past perfect
(+ Past
simple)
action before another action
had
(+ 3rd verb) been / seen

Past continuous
ing
(+ Past simple)
(two actions together)
(while+) was /were ~ing,
(when +)past simple verbs

TYPES OF TENSES

Part of Speech	Types	Position & Function	Form	Example
Tenses (Aspects)		The main verbs are usually positioned between the **subject** and **completion** of active sentences and between **object (subject)** and **subject (completion)** of passive sentences.	subject verb (**tense**) completion.	
	present simple	indicates statements of fact, unchanging situations, routines and programmes.	The be-verb forms are: **am**: used only with the 1st person. **is**: used with the 3rd person, singular common nouns, uncountables nouns & proper nouns. **are**: used with the 2nd person & plurals.	I **am** a teacher. He/She **is** a teacher. That woman **is** a teacher. Gold **is** expensive. Mary **is** a doctor. You **are** welcome. They **are** in the bedroom. The students **are** in class.
			The **main** verb forms are: **base verbs**: used with the 1st person and plurals. Verbs with **s** and **es** endings are used with the 3rd person singular, uncountables & proper nouns.	I **play** tennis. They **play** tennis. The girls **play** tennis. He/She **goes** to school. Water **boils** at 100°. Mary **works** as a doctor.
		It is also used to indicate a routine future action by adding a future time.		The train **leaves** tomorrow morning. (future)

tense	description	form	examples
present continuous	Anything that can be seen or heard *at the moment* can be expressed in the present continuous form; it indicates that the action is not permanent, it will change; it can also be used to express a future action by adding a future time to the sentence. **Now** and **at the moment** are used to emphasis the present moment.	subject present simple **be-verb** **main verb+ing** completion. **Note**: there are often changes to the spelling of the main verbs.	I am **sitting** in the class. The girl **is** **reading** a book. I am **returning** to my country next week.
present perfect	This can be tricky. Basically it indicates actions in the past without indicating a specific time (indicates an experience); indicates the beginning of an action but not its completion; indicates the duration of an action (in the past); indicates actions that take place in unfinished time. The prepositions **since** and **for** are often used with these sentences.	subject **have/has 3rd/past** **participle** [regular (~ed) or irregular (new word)] completion.	I have **bought** a car. (no specific time). She **has lived** in New Zealand *since* 1980. I **have lived** in Iran *for* 30 years. (I'm not in Iran anymore.) The students **have talked** to the teacher *today*.
present perfect continuous	This indicates that an action which started in the past is still occurring in the present; and there is a likelihood that it may continue into the future; the prepositions **since** and **for** may also be used with these sentences; however, when the **here** and **now** coincide, both the present perfect and the present perfect continuous convey the same time period.	subject **have/has 3rd/past** **participle be- verb continuous** **verb** completion. The be-verb is constant; i.e. **been**.	She **has been living** here since she was a child. The students **have been learning** English for two months. She **has lived** *here* for 20 years. She **has been living** *here* for 20 years. They **have learned** English for 2 months. (unfinished time) They **have been learning** English for 2 months. (and still are)

	Explanation	Structure	Examples
past simple	suggests a completed action. The past simple sentence is identified by the presence of a **specific past time** within the discourse; either in the question or statement preceding it or in the statement itself. Words such as **ago** and **last** are past time indicators identify these sentences.	**past simple aux subject base-verb** completion (**past time phrase**)? subject **past simple** completion (**past time phrase**).	**Did** you **go** to the movies **last night?** Yes, I did. I **went** to the movies **last night.** They **came here 5 days ago.**
past continuous	is used to indicate a coinciding of two actions in the past; the past continuous is seldom used on its own. It is generally 'wed' to the past simple with the conjunctions **'while'** or **'when'**. The past continuous acts as a blanket that contains another shorter action (the past simple) or to put it another way; the past continuous is the bigger picture within which there is another picture. Other combinations are also possible. How these time frames relate is up to the narrator. These sentences can be inverted.	subject **past continuous** completion **conj** subject **past simple** completion. **conj** subject **past continuous** completion subject **past simple** completion.	I **was talking** to my lawyer **when** you **saw** me. **When** the phone rang, I **was watching** TV. **While** I **was studying** at university, I **enjoyed** doing theatre. I **enjoyed** doing theatre **while** I **was studying** at university.
past perfect	The past perfect indicates an occurrence before another more recent event. It might also suggest a late realization that the action one is engaged in might be a repeat of a previous action (confusing, eh?). If the conjunctions **before** or **after** are used these sentences may be used in the past simple.	subject **had 3ʳᵈ/past participle** [regular (~ed) or irregular (new word)] subject **past simple** completion.	I **had seen** the film on the plane back to Auckland. I realized I **had seen** this film on the plane back to Auckland. They **had lived** (*lived*) on a farm *before* they came to the city. They moved to a farm *after* they **had lived** (*lived*) in the city.

past perfect continuous	The past perfect continuous sentence, like the past continuous, is seldom used on its own. The conjunctions **when** and **while** are also used here; as can **before, after** and **then**.	subject **had 3rd/past participle be-verb continuous main verb** completion.	I **had been living** (*was living*) in Iran **when** I began to teach English. **While** he **had been studying** (*was studying*) in Spain, he learned to speak Spanish. He had been waiting for 2 hours **before** he remembered that the bus drivers were on strike. Peter had been sitting quietly for a while, **then** suddenly he stood up and left.
future	The English language doesn't really have a future construct; it has intentions but they only become concrete future when a future time is added. The most common construct for future sentences is the *present continuous+future time*.	The future is formed by adding future time to the sentence with words such as; *tomorrow, next, in - - time*, etc. So statements such as; *'I will see you'; 'I'm going to see you'* are only indications of intent; they need a future time to make them true future.	I will see you **tomorrow**. They are going to leave New Zealand **in ten days time**. She is sitting her exam **next** week. The train leaves at 10.00 am **tomorrow**. They are hoping to buy the house **by the end of this year.**

Assisting (helping) verbs				
		These words also assist in suggesting a time frame.		
	auxiliary	indicate present, past, continuous or future times.	See pages 34 and 82.	I am leaving. (now) I was leaving when the phone rang. (past) I am leaving tomorrow. (future)
	modals	The modals can also affect the time frame of the sentence.	See pages 40 and 91.	I can see the car. (now) I can see you tomorrow. I will see you soon. I would play a lot of tennis when I was in college. I would have bought that car if I had the money.
	semi-modals	Semi-modals being verbs have all the characteristics of verbs. With the exception of ought to	See pages 44 and 94.	I want to visit Spain. I want to visit Spain next year. I wanted to visit Spain.

NEGATIVE SENTENCES No/not

In English, generally, there are two main ways of conveying negative information; by the use of the adverb **not** *and the adjective* **no.**

Not *is more often used in its contracted form* **n't** *and is joined to the end of auxiliary verbs and modals. Look at these sentences.*

I do**n't** have a car. I have**n't** got a car.
I have **not** got a car.
This car was **not** made in Spain.
The full form of **not** *is more emphatic.*

No *is more often put before common nouns, usually plurals and uncountables. So;*

I have **no** money.
Sorry, I have **no** time at the moment.

However, there are other ways to show negation; prefixes such as **non, anti, dis**, *etc., and suffixes such as* **less** *indicate a negative concept.* Look *at these sentences.*

This is a **non**-smoking area. Quakers are **anti**-war.
I **dis**like bullies.

When the negative is used in the question form, there are three interpretations possible.
One is a purely negative question enquiring after an action not done. Look at these sentences.

Who **didn't** you see at the party? Where **didn't** you go?

Two, with **Why**, *is that of suggestion:*

Why **not** go to the movies tonight?
Why do**n't** we go to the movies tonight?

Three, that of 'unfulfilled' expectation:

Are**n't** you a teacher? Are**n't** you hungry?

The short, **Why not?** *can also imply agreement:*

Would you like to go to the cinema tonight? **Why not**? Can my little sister come along? **Why not**?

Never *and* **(n't) ever** *also negate the sentence.*

They have **never** eaten fish and chips. They have**n't ever** eaten fish and chips.

PART 3
Explanation of the Parts of speech

ADJECTIVES

Adjectives are words that add information to common nouns so the common nouns can be seen as different from one another; the use of colours is a good example.

In English, adjectives are put before the common noun; i.e. **green** *door; after be-verbs; i.e. I am* **happy**; *and also as gerunds after the common noun in relative sentences; i.e. The man* **standing** *is a well-known writer. This type of adjective is usually followed by a phrase, the sentence could read: The man* **standing by the window** *is a well-known writer; and is a truncated form of a relative clause, so the whole sentence could read:*

The man **who is standing by the window** *is a well-known writer.*

Adjectives are also used to compare things or persons or animals, etc; these are known as
comparative *adjectives. They can also be used as **base** adjectives. Look at these sentences.*

My friend, Peter, is **taller than** I* am.
Reading a book is **more interesting than** watching a movie. He is a **happier** person (than he was) since he married her.
Now it is more usual to use the object pronoun. My friend. Peter, is taller than **me.**

And there are forms of the adjectives that make an object or person unique; these are known as
superlative *adjectives.*

Mount Everest is **the highest** mountain in the world.

This chart should give an idea of how they are formed.

BASE	COMPARATIVE		SUPERLATIVE	
base	*~er than*	*more + base + than*	*the ~est*	*the most + base*
able**	abler	able	ablest	able
beautiful		beautiful		beautiful
big	bigger		biggest	
careful		careful		careful
fine	finer		finest	
nice	nicer		nicest	
cold	colder		coldest	
easy	easier		easiest	
fast	faster		fastest	
friendly**	friendlier	friendly	friendliest	friendly
happy **	happier	happy	happiest	happy
horrible		horrible		horrible

** *All four adjectival forms are possible; there are others as well.*

OTHER TYPES OF ADJECTIVES

*There are also adjectives formed by using the ~**ed** form of a verb, which tend to express a feeling or a state as in; tir**ed**, bor**ed**, etc.*
*And there are adjectives formed by adding ~**ing** to a verb, which then tend to express an opinion as in; interest**ing**, bor**ing**, etc.*

~ed adjectives

These sentences often look just like passive sentences. The difference is in using an action verb or a descriptive verb.

The chair was **placed** in the corner. *(Here **placed** is an action verb)*
The chair **placed** in the middle is for the teacher. *(Here **placed** is an adjective)*

~ing adjectives (gerund adjectives)

These adjectives look just like the continuous verb; however, they do not describe an action.

That was an **interesting** book.
The story was **interesting**.

3ʳᵈ/past participles (regular and irregular verbs)

We can also use the 3ʳᵈ/past participle verbs to express a state such as; **broken, lost, exhausted**, *etc. Look at these sentences:*

The **broken** window hasn't been fixed yet.
The **lost** boy was found sleeping under a bridge.
The **exhausted** child fell asleep on the floor.

See Truncated relative sentences on page 177.

Adjectival suffixes

*These are small units of words attached to the end of nouns and some verbs to convert them into adjectives. For instance; sleep+**y** = sleep**y**; comfort+**able** = comfort**able**.**

*Note: *some words take ~**ible** rather than ~**able**; e.g. sense. In these cases the base word changes; from sense → sens**ible**; whereas with ~**able** the* *base word does not change; break* → *break**able**. When uncertain, using* ~**able** *is a better bet.*

Negative adjective

No *is put before common nouns, both abstract and concrete, to indicate the absence of the nouns. For instance;* **No** *man is an island. They have* ***no*** *money, etc.*

See page 63 and 158 for more on negatives.

ADJECTIVE ORDER

There are eight kinds of adjectives; and they are, generally, used in the order presented, after determiners;

Determiners: a, the, my, your, this, that, etc

1. *Opinion:* lovely, beautiful, expensive, dangerous
2. *Size:* big, small, long, short
3. *Age:* old, new, modern, ancient, 10-year*-old
4. *Shape:* round, oval, fat, skinny
5. *Colour:* red, blue, black, green
6. *Origin:* Chinese, Indian, Kiwi
7. *Material / condition:* cotton, leather, plastic, paper / used, worn, broken.
8. *Purpose* (compound): swimming, washing, coffee.

Note: *adjectives don't usually become plurals.*

And finally the common noun you want to describe.

I have these boots. *(ok, so what?)*
I have these riding boots. *(better)*
I have these leather, riding boots. *(interesting)*
I have these Indian, leather, riding boots. *(more interesting)*
I have these black, Indian, leather, riding boots. *(even more interesting)*
I have these high, black, Indian, leather, riding boots. *(and so on...)*
I have these new, high, black, Indian, leather, riding boots. I have these lovely, new, high, Indian, leather, riding boots.

Of course, not all these types of adjectives need be used to describe one thing, but the order should be maintained, This is pure convention rather than any hard and fast rule.

Actually, it's fun to see how many you can fit in; try it!

ADJECTIVE ORDER

Determiner	Value Opinion	Size *	Age	Shape*	Colour	Origin	Material Condition	Compound Purpose	Noun
a	lovely	big	old	round	black	Kiwi	cotton	coffee	boots
the	beautiful	small	new	long	red	Chinese	leather	tea	shirt
my	ugly	large	next year's	oval	green	British	plastic	swimming	house
Jane's	dangerous	enormous	ancient	rectangular	purple	Indian	woollen	riding	car
Peter's	dirty	tiny	modern	broad	mauve	Canadian	paper	washing	curry
your	expensive	huge	recent	wide	pink	Bulgarian	copper	badminton	sheet
that	untidy	heavy	last year's	square	white	Samoan	steel	tennis	machine
their	cheap	light	15th century	triangular	orange	Maori	used	bed	fish
an	interesting	skinny	10-year-old	fat	blue	French	worn	4 wheel drive	racquet
those	hot	fat	future	slim	grey/gray	Romanian	broken	racing	computer

* Size and shape are interchangeable.

Obviously not to be read across in a straight line, but there's always room for some hilarity.

ADVERBS

There are six types of adverbs; they can be generally recognized by their ~ly endings which are usually attached to the end of adjectives.

of comment

These adverbs are usually put at the beginning of the sentence and express an opinion or feeling; the most common adverbs are: **personally**, **generally**, **fortunately**. *Look at these sentences.*

> **Personally**, I don't care for cowboy movies.
> **Fortunately**, the accident did not cause serious damage.

of manner

These adverbs are usually put after the main verb or at end of the sentence. They define how an action is performed. Sometimes they may be seen before the main verb. Look at these sentences.

> He walked **slowly** down the street.
> He walked down the street **slowly**.
> He **quickly** left the room.

CAREFUL: *Not all words ending in ~ly are adverbs.*

> The **elderly*** gentleman walked **slowly** up the stairs.
> The **friendly*** woman patted my dog **affectionately**.
> ***These are not adverbs!**

of frequency

These adverbs are usually put before the main verb and indicate the frequency of the action and answer the question 'How often ...?'

> They **always** come to class late.
> They are **always** talking in class.
> They have **never** been to Spain.

of degree

These adverbs are usually put before adjectives or adverbs to vary the intensity of the adjective or adverb. However, there are adjectives which already express the peak of their intensity and therefore cannot be further graded. **Excellent** *and* **perfect** *are examples of such words; also most superlative adjectives cannot be graded. Look at these sentences.*

The coffee is **too** hot to drink.
The test was **pretty** easy.
The teacher spoke **quite** slowly.
~~That was a **very** perfect example.~~

time and time phrases

Time adverbs can be put at the beginning of a sentence followed by a comma* or at the end of the sentence. These can be dates, years, clock times, etc. Words like **ago, next, last, yesterday, tomorrow** *all indicate the time of the action. Look at these sentences.*

I'll see you **at 6.00 pm.**
My birthday is **on the 30th of December.**
Several weeks ago, they left New Zealand.

*Note: some people might not agree.

place and place phrases

Place adverbs can be put at the beginning of the sentence followed by a comma or at the end of the sentence. These are preceded by prepositions, articles, possessive pronouns, etc. These can be a variety of places such as: cities, countries; locations such as: cinema, bus stop, etc. Look at these sentences.

I'll meet you **at the cinema.**
They got off the bus **at the end of the street.**
The picture was hanging **on the wall.**
At the end of the street, there was a beautiful old house.

Then there are adverb CLAUSES

These are full sentences following words such as; **when, before after,** *etc.*

almost and most

The use of these two adverbs can be quite confusing to some learners. **Almost** *infers* **nearly** *or* **not quite, not meeting expectations.** *It can be put before* **adjectives, numbers** *and* **main verbs.** *Look at these sentences.*

> I was **almost** late for class. *(When I got there the lecture had not begun.)*
> I have **almost $5.00.** *(Just slightly less than $5.0.)*
> I **almost** missed the bus. *(The bus was about to leave when I got to it.)*

Most *can have the same connotation as* **very** *or* **majority.** *It can be put before* **adjectives, adverbs**
and **plural common nouns.** *look at these sentences.*

> It was a **most** interesting film.
> She spoke **most** persuasively.
> **Most** people tend to be polite.

ADVERB CHART

COMMENT	MANNER	FREQUENCY	DEGREE	TIME	PLACE
personally generally surprisingly strangely fortunately unfortunately curiously at least sadly happily naturally	quietly slowly carefully beautifully noisily badly kindly lazily gracefully calmly foolishly fast/hard	always frequently usually often sometimes seldom hardly ever never ~n't ever once twice	quite so pretty rather too extremely really	clock times dates now at this moment yesterday today tomorrow _____ago last/this: week, month, year, decade, century, the____before the____after	here there downtown in the cinema at home on the bus any place
and many more	**and many more**	**and many more**	**and many more**	**and many more**	**and many more**

ADVERBS of FREQUENCY These %s are only a rough guide.	%	ADVERBS of DEGREE These are the more common ones and are not related to the %s on the left.
always	100	a bit
nearly/almost always	90	a little
usually	80	slightly
very often/frequently	70	quite
often	60	pretty
sometimes	50	rather
occasionally	40	very
seldom	20	so
almost never	10	extremely
never/n't ever	0	too (gives a negative meaning)
		There are many of these.

adverbs with present perfect

There are six adverbs most commonly used with the present perfect structure; these are; **already***,* **just***,* **never***,* **(n't) ever***,* **still** *and* **yet***. These adverbs are also used in other tenses.*

adverbs	meaning
already	indicates that an action has been done before the query regarding it.
just	indicates the action was done relatively recently; keyword – relatively.
never	not in one's life; suggests something possible not being done.

(n't) ever	same as 'never, but used in negative or question sentences.
still	indicates that an expected action has passed its due time.
yet	indicates that an expected action is expected to happen.

Already, just, never *and* **(n't) ever** *are put between the* **auxiliary verb** *and the* **3ʳᵈ/past participle. Ever** *is used in negative and question sentences.* **Already** *can also be put at the end of the sentence.* **Still** *is put before the* **negative auxiliary verb** *and* **yet** *is put at the end of negative and question sentences.*

already

'Please give me your homework.'
'We have] **already** [given it to you **(already)**.'
'Would you like a cup of coffee?'
'No thank you. I've] **already** [had one **(already)**.'

In both conversations the action was done **before** *the offer or request.*

just

This is tricky in terms of the length of time passed since the action was performed - has a touch of Einstein's Theory of Relativity.

Would you like some coffee?
Thank you, but I've] **just** [had some.

This could imply that I had some coffee a few moments ago, certainly within that day; the effect of the coffee is still with me; I don't need any more.

When are you going to buy a car?
I can't. I've] **just** [bought a house.

This could imply any length of time; I'm still paying off the mortgage. The purchase of the house might have been several months ago.

never

This is used to indicate that one has not done something in the entire length of one's life. It can also indicate that something that is close at hand, convenient and easy to perform was not done.

My wife has] **never** [smoked.

This sentence contains two messages; one, she has not smoked in her entire life; two, while smoking is not beyond her reach: cigarettes are available everywhere (close at hand, convenient, easy), nevertheless she has resisted the practice.

I have] **never** [been to Stewart Island.

Stewart Island is a part of New Zealand, just south of South Island, a half hour or at most a couple of hours by air from anywhere in New Zealand. I have lived in New Zealand for a long time, I have been almost everywhere else but the island which is close, convenient and easy to reach; I haven't been there; hence, the use of **never.**
The Antarctic is not accessible to everyone, so there is no need to use **never**:
I haven't been to the Antarctic *should suffice.*

(n't) ever

This adverb has the same connotation as **never**, *however, it is used in negative sentences, hence the*
(n't); *and question sentences, so we can say;*

I have] **n't ever** [eaten spinach.
Or ask;
Have you] **ever** [eaten spinach?

still

This adverb suggests that something that was expected to happen by a specified time hasn't happened. So the sentence is usually in the negative form. Peter should have been here at 9.00 am. It is now 9.30 but he isn't here; so we can say:

Peter] **still** [hasn't arived.

yet

This adverb suggests that there is an expectation or intention to do something in the future. It is not accomplished at the moment, hence the sentence is in the negative.

I haven't had lunch] **yet**.

This means that at some point in the future I intend to have lunch.

Have you had lunch] **yet**?

The question suggests that there is an expectation that you will be having lunch at some point (in the future) or that the time for having lunch is around now.

Negative adverb

Not *is only connected to the end of auxiliary verbs and modals in its abbreviated form,* ***n't****, but not often to main verbs. In its full form,* ***not****, it adds emphasis to the statement.*
*For instance; He is****n't*** *a teacher./He is* ***not*** *a teacher; He ca****n't*** *dance./He can* ***not*** *dance.*

See page 63 for more on negatives.

ARTICLES

Every sentence should have an article, a possessive pronoun or a demonstrative pronoun. Articles are put before <u>initial</u> singular, common nouns.

Articles are also put before adjectives when they are combined with common nouns.

Articles are not put before <u>initial</u> uncountable nouns or plural nouns. Hence, referred to as the **zero (some)** *article.*

There are two singular articles, **a** *and* **an***, commonly known as the indefinite articles, and one definite article* **THE** *in the written form which has two pronunciations governed by the sound (word) that follows them; '**thuh**' (/ðə/) before CONSONANT SOUNDS and '**thee**' (/ði:/) before VOWEL SOUNDS.* **a** *(uh/əi/) and* **an** *(/æn/) are used when a noun is mentioned for the first time; they indicate that the object is one of many and is not object specific.* **An** *when spoken joins the following word with an emphasis on the* **N***, e.g.* **aNegg, aNelephant***, etc.* **The** *is object specific and has approximately 26 uses. The most common use of **the** is in reference to an object (noun) mentioned for the second and subsequent times.*

The **zero (some)** *article or invisible article simply means that no article is put before plural common nouns and uncountable common nouns when these words are used for the first time.* **Some** *is becoming a frequent replacement for the* **zero** *article. Look at these sentences.*

There is **a** book on the table.
The book belongs to me. *(same book referred to a second time)*
There is water in the glass. *(no article)*
The water is cold. *(the water mentioned above)*
I was looking at (some) books in the library.
The books were on New Zealand history.

Articles are not generally used with pronouns and proper nouns, but there are occasions when they are; here are a couple of instances:

There's **a** Mr. Jones to see you.
Is that **the (thee/ði:/)** Mr. Jones?

A: Someone's on the phone for you.

B: Is it **a** he or **a** she?

Words such as **hospital**, **hotel** *and* **hospice** *may use either* **a** *or* **an** *before them when spoken, however, it is preferred that* **an** *is used when these words are written. Your choice.*

the ['thuh' (/ðə/) and 'thee' (/ði:/)]

It is used in a variety of ways: the most common use is:

1. when the same common noun is used for the second and subsequent times in the same discourse.

Other uses are:

	USE	EXAMPLES
2	to indicate that there is only one in existence, with the exception of 'God'	the sea, the sky, the moon, the sun, the stars
3	to indicate that only one exists in a specific context	the king, the queen, the president, the capital, the God of
4	to indicate well-known names or professions	'thee' (/ði:/) Steinbeck, 'thee'(/ði:/) writer
5	when proper nouns are used as adjectives	the Auckland weather, the Bangkok traffic
6	mountain ranges, rivers, falls,	the Himalayas, the Alps, the Nile, the Angel Falls
7	ordinal numbers	the first, the second, the third
8	dates	the first of April, the sixth of May
9	directions	to the right, to the left
10	compass points	to the south, to the north-east
11	positions	the top, the middle, the centre, the bottom
12	superlatives	the biggest, the most, the best
13	musical instruments	the saxophone, the piano, the rums
14	adjectives used as nouns	the good, the bad, the ugly
15	generic public places	the cinema, the opera, the hospital, the airport
16	countries which are 'plural'	the USA, the Emirates, the UK
17	nationalities	the British, the Chinese, the Koreans
18	most newspaper titles	the Herald, the New York Times
19	the media	the radio, the newspapers, the internet
20	parts of the body (possessive pronouns are more common)	the nose, the shoulder, the eyes
21	seasons (optional)	the winter, the summer, the spring
22	'whole' family names	the Smiths, the Lees, the Browns
23	decades	the 1920s, the 1950s, the 1990s
24	these words (and more)	end, last, same, beginning, start, truth, next
25	specific groups of people	the police, the army, the navy, the military
26	parts of day	the morning, the afternoon, the evening, the night, the weekend

AUXILIARY VERBS

There are three types of auxiliary verbs; be-verbs, 'invisible' (dummy) verbs and perfect verbs. Auxiliary verbs function as both 'helping' and main verbs. All three types are used in forming question and negative sentences. The invisible auxiliary verb has the added characteristic of placing emphasis when put before the main verb; she **does** sing well.

The auxiliary be-verbs and the auxiliary perfect verbs are visible; they are seen in the sentence, however, the invisible auxiliary verbs, **do, does** *and* **did** *are not. So this becomes a difficult concept for those whose language allows the main verb to become negative.*

The be-verbs; **am, is, are,** *when used as main verbs imply the existence of things and persons; their characteristics, etc. For instance,* There **is** a tree in the garden; There **are** five people in the room; Peter **is** a doctor, *etc. These can be converted to the question and negative forms;* **Am** I a teacher? **Is** today Monday? I'**m not** a teacher, Today **isn't** Monday.

These types of sentences are known as present simple sentences.

Am not *is not contracted to* **amn't***; in some cases it is replaced by* **aren't***; for example;* I'm a teacher, **aren't** I? *And then we have* **ain't** *which like the Indian* **isn't it?** *covers almost every conceivable abbreviated auxiliary negative verb;* am not, is not, are not, have not, etc: I **ain't** a teacher, He **ain't** a teacher, We **ain't** eaten yet. *This use is strictly colloquial (in spoken form) and is not recommended for formal use, particularly in writing.*

The simple past be-verbs; **was, were** *imply that things might not be so now. At some point in the past the situation might have been true.* There **was** a tree in the garden; There **were** five people in the room; Peter **was** a doctor. *These situations might not be true now. These types of sentences are known as past simple sentences.*

When the be-verbs **am, is, are** *are used with a main verb, the main verb takes on an –***ing** *ending and this combination implies a 'nowness'. The action is taking place at the moment, suggesting a temporariness, the situation will change. So;* 'I **am writing**', *puts the time of this action in the present and suggests that I will not be writing for long. These types of sentences are known as present simple continuous.*

However, when a future time is added to the sentence, the action moves into the future, so: 'I **am leaving** tomorrow' *puts the action into the future.*

When the be-verbs **was** *and* **were** *are combined with the ~***ing** *main verb they imply that an action envelopes another action or occurs simultaneously. These sentences are usually accompanied by another sentence, therefore there are usually two sentences referring to two actions. They might also imply that two separate actions were occurring coincidentally*. These sentences are joined by the words* **when** *and* **while**. *So;* 'I **was walking** down the street **when** I saw the accident.'; 'I saw the accident **while** I **was walking** down the street.'

*I **was reading** a book **while** the children **were sleeping**.

These types of sentences are known as past simple continuous.

Do & does, *when used as main verbs show that some action is habitually carried out. For instance,* 'He **does** the cooking'; 'I **do** the dishes'; ***did*** *expresses one single action done at a specific time in the past*; 'She **did** her homework before going to bed'. *Unlike the be-verbs they cannot be used as questions or turned into negative words, they become the auxiliary verbs and the main verb remains as* **do.** *For instance,* '**Does** he **do** the cooking?', 'No, I **don't do** the cooking.';' **Did** she **do** her homework?' *And not* '**Do** he the cooking?', 'No, I **don't** the cooking.'; **Did** she her homework?'

They are referred to as 'invisible' because they are **not** *seen in the positive sentences. To help my students remember their use I refer to present and past simple sentences as a pregnant woman waiting to give birth to* **do, does** *and* **did** *in the event these sentences need to be used as question or negative sentences. This prevents students from transforming the main verbs into question or negative forms.*

Have, has, had *in the first instance show that something is in possession of something else, but there are other implications as well. As main verbs these words can be converted to question or negative forms in two ways. They can be like the be-verbs and they can be like the invisible verbs. The quaint forms are:* **Have** you any children? They **haven't** any money, She **hadn't** any time. *These forms are not in frequent use these days. The modern usage is:* **Does** he **have** any children? They **don't have** any money? She **didn't have** any time.

When **have** *and* **has** *are combined with the* **3rd/past participle**, *in either the* **~ed** *or new word* (**irregular**) *form, this combination implies a life experience or action taken in unspecified or unfinished time. For instance,* 'I **have** read Gone with the Wind.'*(experience);* 'They **haven't** had lunch yet.'*(unspecified time);* 'He **has** played football today.'*(unfinished time).*

Note*: The first two sentences don't have a specific time and the third sentence indicates a time that is, at the moment, unfinished.*

These types of sentences are known as present perfect simple. The present perfect is not commonly used in the USA.

Had *combined with the* **3rd/past participle** *suggests a prior action often indicated by the use of* **before** *or* **after**, *so;* He **had** eaten **before** he (had) left the house./He **had** left the house **after** he **had** eaten.

The present perfect simple is quite a difficult concept for most learners of English as a second language.

And while we're at it, here's another use of **have***; implying causing someone or something to do an action. This type of use is called*

CAUSATIVE and the causative verbs are:

have

The grammatical form with **have** *is as follows:*

*Subject+***have***+object+***verb***+2nd object (completion). The different tenses are constructed through the verb* **have***. Look at these sentences.*

My mother **has** us **eat** all our vegetables.
Mary **has** her hair **done** by Antonio.
I **am having** my car **repaired** at Automotive Cars.
The choirmaster **had** us **singing** at the top of our voices.
The rain **had** us **running** for shelter.
The manager will **have** him **arrested**.
Have Peter **give** you a ride. (a suggestion; Ask (request) Peter to give you a ride)
What do you **have** a **need** for?

Here are some similar grammatical structures.

make

The verb **make** *can be used in the same manner. However,* **make** *has a more coercive connotation than* **have** *and is more limited in its grammatical structures. So replacing* **have** *in the sentences above does not work in every instance. As we can see:*

My mother **made** us **eat** our vegetables.
Mary **made** her hair **done** by Antonio. **X**
I **made** my car **repaired** at Automotive Cars. **X**
The choirmaster **made** us **singing** at the top of our voices. **X**
The choirmaster **made** us **sing** at the top of our voices.
The rain **made** us **running** for shelter. **X**
The rain **made** us **run** for shelter.
The manager will **make** him **arrested**. **X**

The grammatical form with **make** *is as follows:*

*Subject+***make***+object+***base-verb***+2nd object (completion). The different tenses are constructed through the verb* **make***. For instance;*

My mother **makes** us **eat** our vegetables.
My mother **is making** us **eat** our vegetables.
My mother **made** us **eat** our vegetables.
My mother **has made** us **eat** our vegetables.
Make the children **eat** their vegetables.

The verb **get** *can be used like the be-verb to make passive sentences like these:*

He **got** arrested.
The injured person **got** taken to hospital.
She **is getting** taken care of by the nurse.

It can also be used to show that a request or persuasion is/was necessary to have something done; the grammatical form is:

*Subject+***get***+person object+***to***+***base-verb***+object (completion). The different tenses are expressed through the verb* **get***. Look at these sentences.*

My mother **got** me **to do** the dishes.
I'm **getting** the students **to rearrange** the classroom.
Get Peter **to give** you a lift.

And we have **let**. **Let** *in this context has the meaning of 'allow' or 'give permission'. The grammatical structure is:*

*Subject+***let***+object+***base-verb***+2ⁿᵈ object (completion). Look at these sentences.*

She **lets** her dogs **sit** on the sofa. They are **letting** us **go** in.
Let them **leave**.

And then we have **need.** *It can be a main verb, a negative modal, and a semi-modal.*

Main verb.

need

I **need** a book.
He **needs** $5.00.
I **don't need** your advice.

Negative modal: has the same implication as **don't have to**.

You **needn't** come to the party.
They **needn't** stay any longer.

It can also be used to form questions.

Need I come to class tomorrow?
Need they bring any food?
Need you talk so loudly?

Semi-modal.

I **need to** buy some clothes.
She **needs to** practise much more.
You don't **need to** come to the party. (has the same implication as **don't have to**)

have vs have got

And here's my pet: the difference between **have** *and* **have got** *[(gotten) US].*
To me **have** *indicates a natural possession, i.e.*

All animals **have** two eyes.
I **have** brown eyes.
A car **has** four wheels.
The forest **has** trees.

Get *means to acquire, to obtain, i.e.* 'I **get** my bread from that bakery';
'Where did you **get** your book from?' 'Who **got** this book for you?', *etc.*

Thus, or should I say, ergo, ***have got*** *indicates that something has been acquired and is external to the possessor. Look at these sentences.*

I **have got** a watch; my watch **has** three hands.
This book **has** 200 hundred pages.
That dog **has got** an expensive collar.
I **have got** a wife and I **have** two children. *(eh?!)*

I hope you appreciate the subtle difference between **have** *and* **have got**. *But who cares anyway. We will all continue to use* **have got** *for both purposes. Perhaps I'm just nit picking.*

Then, of course, we have

have got to

which implies a very forceful obligation. Look at these sentences.

You **have got to** pay your rent on time.
We **have got to** call the police; it looks like something bad is happening.
He **has got to** take his child to the hospital.

Notice the tense/time difference between I **have got** a watch *and* You **have got to** pay your rent on time.

CONJUNCTIONS

Conjunctions are words that make complex sentences by joining two or more sentences to form a collection of ideas.

Conjunctions join sentences:

a.   *with similar ideas*

b.   *with opposing ideas*

c.   *of causes, reasons, purposes, conditions, results or time.*

d.   *They can join adjectives, adverbs, common nouns, proper nouns, verbs, etc.*

e.   *and then there are paired conjunctions*

Here is a chart of the more common conjunctions.

similar	contrast	reason	purpose	conditional****	result	time
and also too as well (as) as if as though	but although (even though) ,however, (in spite of) or despite otherwise whereas (on the other hand)	because as since* so due to in case	so that in case	if unless should had (as long as) provided providing (whether__or not) even if	(so ** that) (such ***that) as a result	when whenever while as soon as until after before since*

*also a preposition; **put an adjective; *** put an adjectival phrase (a good idea, etc).

**** see conditionals on page 144.

There are more complex conjunctions but these should cover most needs. Here are some examples.

Similar ideas:

I bought a book **and** a few DVDs.

They play tennis, they **also** play badminton.

She likes ice cream: he likes ice cream, **too**.

The students, **as well as** the teacher, were* absent.

John was late to class, **so** was Ian.

Albert looked **as if** he were** tired.

Albert looks **as though** he is tired.
The verb should correspond to the subject noun.
were *is usually used instead of* **was** *in 2nd conditional sentences.*

Contrasting ideas:
I like mangoes **but** I don't like apples.
He failed to get the job **although** he presented a very good CV.
She failed the exam **even though** she had worked very hard for it.
We had a wonderful time at the zoo **in spite of** the rain.
We had a wonderful time at the zoo **despite** the rain.
We need to leave now **otherwise** we'll miss the train.
Some countries are lovely to visit; **on the other hand**, they can be quite expensive.
Silk is a soft cloth, **whereas**, burlap is rough.

Reasons:
He went home early **because** he had a headache.
He went home early **since** he had a headache.
He went home early **as** he had a headache.
He had a headache **so** he went home early.
Due to the bad weather, we postponed the match.
I brought an umbrella **in case** it rained.

Purposes:
I hired a car **so that** I could* travel at leisure.
I'll hire a car **so that** I can* travel around New Zealand.
I called my mother **in case** she needed my help.
always use can or could.

Conditionals: (also see page 144)
You should do well **if** you continue to work hard.
You should do well **whether** you work hard **or not**.
You won't do well **even if** you work hard.
You won't do well **unless** you work hard.
You will do well **as long as** you work hard.
You will do well **provided** you work hard.
You will do well **providing** you work hard.
Had you not worked hard, you wouldn't have done well.

Results:

He was **so** <u>angry</u>**that** he went home early.
It was **such** <u>an interesting movie</u>** **that** he took all his friends to it.
It was **such** <u>a wet day</u>** **that** we decided to stay home.
The traffic was very heavy; **as a result** we missed our train.
*always a <u>base </u>adjective in between.** always an adjectival phrase in between.*

Time:

I have a beer **when** I get home.
I am always happy to talk to him **whenever** I see him.
She went up and kissed him **as soon as** she saw him.
We stayed in the restaurant **until/till** it closed.
We left the theatre **after/before** the movie finished.
They have lived in the same place **(ever) since** they came to New Zealand.

Paired conjunctions:

Both my mother **and** my sister are* doctors.
Not only my mother **but** (<u>also</u>) my sister (<u>also</u>)**.** is a doctor
Neither my mother **nor** my sister <u>is</u>*** a doctor.
Neither I **nor** my brother <u>has</u>*** a car.
Neither I **nor** my brothers <u>are</u>*** doctors.
Neither I **nor** my brothers <u>have</u>*** a car.
Neither my brothers **nor** I <u>am</u>*** married.
I'll **either** go to the cinema **or** the theatre.
You can **(either)** have **(either)**** ice cream **or** coke but not both.
* *always the plural form of the verb. ** in either position.*
*** *The verb should correspond to the noun nearest it.*

MODALS

Modals are generally lumped in with the auxiliary verbs, but there is clearly a distinction between them. Auxiliary verbs do not change the basic meaning of the main verb; they merely change the sentence into its negative or question form. Modals, on the other hand, have several significant characteristics; the most important of which is the fact that they cannot be used as main verbs. They give the main verb a slightly different connotation and their tense use is rather complex.

Modals are always followed by a base verb.

While most of the modals have words that look like their past tense; some usage just doesn't make sense; for instance, 'I could see you yesterday' is perfectly correct grammatically, but makes no sense. However, 'I could play very good tennis when I was in high school' does.

Here are some possible uses of the modals.

Can

1st conditional (possibility)	If you like, we **can** go to a movie tonight. We **can** go to a movie tonight if you like.
ability	Harry **can*** dance very well.
possibility	I think you **can*** pass the exam.
permission	Yes, you **can** come in.
request	**Can** I leave now?

see **able to for extended use.*

Could

2nd conditional (low possibility)	I **could** buy a house if I had the money.
3rd conditional (lost opportunity/regret)	If I had had the money, I **could** have bought that house.
past ability (present inability)	Mary **could** play the piano very well when she was a child. *(Maybe she doesn't play it so well now.)*
polite request	**Could** you pass the sugar, please?
past reported speech	She said she **could** visit me tomorrow.
suggestion/possibility	I **could** see you tomorrow.
after 'wish' (regret)	I wish I **could** sing well.

Will

1st conditional (strong desire)	If I have the money, I ('ll) will buy that house.
strong desire to do something	I have the money; I ('ll) will buy that house.
sudden, unexpected decision	'No fish! Ok, I ('ll) will have the steak.'
prediction	I think it ('ll) will rain tomorrow.

Note: *the abbreviated negative form of will is* **won't**.

Would

2nd conditional (not possible at the moment)	If I had the money, I ('d) would buy that house.
3rd conditional (missed opportunity/regret)	If I had had the money, I ('d) would have bought that house.
repeated actions in the past (perhaps discontinued)	I would run 20 kms a day when I played sport. *(Maybe I don't now.)*
past reported speech	He said he would buy that house.
polite offer	Would you like an ice cream?
with 'wish'	He wishes you wouldn't talk so loudly.

May

1st conditional (50/50 possibility)	If I have the money, I may buy that house.
permission	You may leave the room.
request	May I leave the room? *(Preferred to Can)*
average possibility	It may rain this evening.
wish	May you have a wonderful year.

Might

1st conditional (mixed)	If I have the money, I might buy that house.
2nd conditional	Might is not commonly used in the past form.
3rd conditional	If I had had the money, I might have bought that house.
past reported speech	He said he might see you the next day.
possibility (but unlikely)	It might rain this evening. *(But I don't think so.)*
suggestion	Might I suggest you try the fish? *(Not common/formal)*

Shall

| offer with 'I' | Shall I open the door? |
| suggestion with 'we' | Shall we go now? |

Replaced by **'will'** *in other usages.*

Should

1st conditional (mixed)	If you have the money, you **should** buy that house.
1st conditional	If **I should** see him, I**'ll** tell him.
2nd conditional	**Should is not commonly used in the past form.**
3rd conditional (mixed)	If you had (had) the money, you **should** have bought that house.
suggestion	You **should** see that film.
advice	You **should** see a doctor.
strong possibility	He **should** pass the exam.
past reported speech	He said you **should** see a doctor. (**Not** *the past tense of* **shall**.)

Must

1st conditional	If she phones, I **must** tell her.
adherence to law	We **must** pay our taxes.
personal obligation	I must **study** harder.

Note: *Most learners of English come with the idea that modals, like auxiliary verbs, have both present and past tenses. I think it is a good idea to teach each modal as a separate entity.*

SEMI-MODALS

Semi-modals are so called because they sit in the same place in the sentence as do the modals. However, since they are made up of verbs plus the prepositions 'to' they can sometimes combine with modals, as in **would like to.**

Like the modals they are always followed by base verbs and like modals they change the meaning of the main verb somewhat. For instance; 'I visit Spain', suggests a routine or habit, whereas, 'I'm going to visit Spain' changes the meaning to a future intention.

Keep in mind that semi-modals are a combination of verbs plus 'to' so they can be, in some cases, used in different tenses and have all the characteristics of verbs. For instance;

They **dared to** touch the tiger.
She is **hoping to** buy a house soon.
He **wants to** go home early.
Etc.

Here are the more common semi-modals and their meaning.

be-verb+able to	have the skill, but suggests some degree of difficulty; not entirely similar to 'can'.*
dare to	take the risk, be brave, have the courage.
be-verb+going to	have a strong intention to do something.
have to	strong obligation to do something you might not want to do, usually from external pressure.
hope to	a wish.
like to	enjoy doing.
need to	a necessity to do something.
ought to	an obligation, similar in use to 'should'.
plan to	think about doing something.
be-verb+supposed to	intended 'plan'.
used to	custom, habit, behaviour in one's past.
want to	a personal wish.
would like to	almost like 'want to', but it's an intention for the future.

There are more but these should be enough for everyday use.

*Look at these sentences.

Harry **can** dance very well. *Here the speaker is appreciating Harry's skill at dancing.*

Harry is **able to** walk. *Here the speaker is mentioning the degree to which Harry can walk. Harry may be a toddler; Harry may be getting over an illness, etc.*

I **can** come to the party. *There is no impediment to my coming to the party.*

I am **able to** come to the party. *I have removed any impediment preventing me from coming to the party.*

*The use of **can** or **able to** requires some consideration.*

NOUNS

Nouns are basically the name of things and there are four kinds: **abstract**, *which name things that are not tangible, like feelings;* **common** *(concrete), which are the collective names for similar things, like* **table, chair, boy**, *etc;* **proper**, *which are names given to specific things and do not usually have a collective quality, such as names of people, cities, countries, etc. These words always begin with a capital letter. And finally* **gerunds**, *which are continuous verbs without the use of the be-verb, i.e, playing, swimming, shopping, etc.*

Nouns can be both the **subject** *and* **object** *of a sentence.*

Here are some nouns

Nouns	Words such as;
abstract	happiness, opportunity, intelligence, fascination, ability, etc.
common	man, woman, cats, dogs, chair, cars, etc.
proper	Peter, Mary, Brazil, Auckland, River Nile, etc.
gerunds	swimming, shopping, walking, etc.

Look at these sentences.

Abstract.
Everyone seeks **happiness**.
Intelligence is not as common as we think.
'It was **fascination**, I know ...'

Common (concrete).
The **teacher** is talking to a **student**.
A **student** is talking to the **teacher**.
The **boy** ran off with the **ball**.

Proper.
Peter has gone to **Brazil**.
Auckland is the largest city in **New Zealand**.
Mary is going to marry **Peter**.

Gerunds.
I enjoy **playing** tennis.
The Art Gallery has some very good **paintings**.
Swimming, **dancing** and **boxing** are very good exercises.

PREFIXES

These are small units of words or sub-words which are attached to the beginning of other words. The main word then undergoes a change in meaning, more often the new meaning is the opposite of the original meaning. Prepositions and adverbs may be used as prefixes as well. Some prefixes are joined with a hyphen; some aren't.

Here are some common prefixes and their meaning with examples.

prefixes	meaning	examples
a, il, im, in, ir, non, un, dis	reverse the meaning of the original word.	atypical, illegal, impatient, irregular, non- smoker, unpack, disbelief.
ante-	prior, before or in front of.	ante-chamber, antenatal, antedate.
anti, counter	oppose, opposite, be against.	anti-war, anti-abortion, counter-terrorist, anticlockwise.
auto	operate by itself, do by self.	automatic, autobiography.
bi	twice in a given time, having two of.	bi-annual, bilingual, bicycle.
co	combining with, together.	co-author, cooperate, co-owner.
ex	no longer the same, former.	ex-husband, ex-prisoner, ex-teacher.
macro	large.	macro-society, macroeconomics.
micro	very small.	microchip, microclimate, microbe.
mini	small.	mini-skirt, mini-golf, mini-series.
mal	put together badly, not work, evil	malformed, maladjusted, malfunction, malevolent.
mis	do badly or wrongly.	misheard, misbehave, misuse.
mono	only one, single.	monolingual, monorail, monotone.
multi	consist of many.	multi-storey, multi-cultural, multi-faceted, multilingual.
over	too much, more than necessary.	over-priced, over-cook, over-weight.
post	after an event.	post-war, postpone, postgraduate.
pre	before an event.	pre-dawn, pre-existed, pre-war.
pro	support, be on the side of, agree with.	pro-democracy, pro-choice, pro-abortion.
pseudo	fake, false, artificial.	pseudo-science, pseudonym.
re	repeat, do again, return to a former state.	rewrite, return, re-do, regrow.
semi	half, not complete, less than.	semi-circle, semi-final, semi-precious.
sub, under	under or below, not quite, smaller.	sub-standard, subhuman, underwear, underdog, sub-zero, undergraduate.
super	larger than usual; very good.	supermarket, supermodel, superhero.

There are other prefixes but these should suffice for now.

'a' as a PREFIX

There are a few instances when 'a' is used as a prefix; in these instances the 'a' reverses the original meaning of the word it is attached to; here are some such words; taken from Cambridge International Dictionary of English, Proctor, P (Ed in Chief), 2001, UK, CUP.

CAREFUL: *Not all words beginning with an 'a' reverse the meaning of the original word; words such as:* **aback**, **abase**, **aground**, **around**, *etc.*

Base word	Meaning	Meaning with prefix 'a'
moral	p.917: relating to the standards of good or bad behaviour, etc.	p.42: without moral principles.
part	p.1028: some but not all of a thing; a piece which combines with other pieces, etc.	p.52/53: separated; except for, not considering, etc.
political	p.1092: relating to politics.	p.54: not interested or connected with anything political.
septic	p.1295: infected by bacteria, etc.	p.67: medically clean or without infection.
sexual	p. 1303 adjective pertaining to sex.	p.67: without sex, sexual organs, not interested in sexual relationships.
symmetrical	p.1480: the quality of having parts that match each other, etc.	p.75: with two sides, parts or halves which are not exactly the same, etc.
theist	p.1508: one who believes that there is only one God.	p.76: someone who believes that God or gods do not exist.
tonal	p.1534: music that is based on major and minor keys.	Not mentioned in this dictionary. However, means lacking a tonal centre or established key.
typical	p. 1576: a particular group of people or things which share similar characteristics, etc.	p.78: different from all the others of its type.

Here are some sentences using the 'a' prefix.

Habitual criminals are likely to be **amoral**.
My son took his radio **apart**.
Apolitical people do a disservice to their country.
If you cut your finger, you should use an **aseptic** lotion.
Some living creatures are **asexual**.
Most human faces are **asymmetrical**.
Atheism is increasing in the west.
For the western ear **atonal** music is not easy to listen to.
Her way of thinking is **atypical** of Asian women.

SUFFIXES

These are small units of words or sub-words which are attached to the end of other words. When this is done the original word changes its form from **adjective** *to* **adverb** *(slow to* slowly*) or* **verb** *to* **noun** *(teach to* teacher*), etc; however, in most cases it retains the characteristic of the main word. Suffixes are generally joined to the end of the word without the use of a hyphen and might also undergo some changes in spelling.*

Here are some common suffixes, and their meaning and examples.

suffixes	meaning	examples
er, or	having an occupation.	teacher, actor, engineer.
ist	having an occupation.	scientist, artist, chemist.
er, ian, ese, ish	belonging to a city, nationality.	Londoner, Russian, Chinese, English.
ish	having a quality or quantity of	reddish, foolish, fiveish (5ish).
hood	belonging to, stages of age.	neighbourhood, childhood.
ship	containing the characteristic of.	friendship, relationship.
ocracy	containing the characteristic of.	autocracy, democracy.
ful	having the quality or quantity of.	beautiful, fistful, roomful, useful.
ly, like	having the quality of.	slowly, politely, birdlike, childlike.
ness, ity	having the quality of.	happiness, rarity.
y	having the quality of.	noisy, sleepy, creamy.
less	not having, lacking, without.	helpless, childless, timeless.
al, (t)ic, ive, ous	forms adjectives; having the quality of.	national, heroic, active, humorous.
able, ible, ed, ish, esque	forms adjectives; having the quality of.	comfortable, forcible, tired, picturesque.
ism	a philosophy, belief.	Catholicism, Hinduism, idealism.
ant, ation, al	changes verbs into nouns.	inhabitant, exploration, denial.
ment,	changes verbs into nouns.	government, enjoyment.
ion	changes verbs to nouns.	imagination, violation.
age	resultant, state.	breakage, bondage.
ee	indicates the non-active person.	employee, interviewee, trainee.
ing	changes verbs into nouns or adjectives gerunds, or continuous verb forms.	swimming, shopping, is swimming, is shopping, etc.
ify, ize (ise), en	to cause.	signify, dramatize, sadden.
ward(s), wise	in the direction of, manner.	forward, clockwise.
The suffix, **ess,** to denote the female form of a profession is now being discarded in some instances, e.g., actor, doctor, etc.		

There are other suffixes but these should suffice for now.

PREPOSITIONS

They usually come immediately after the main verb and/or the first object in the completion. E.g. I come **to** school **by** bus.

They 'join' the verb to the object (completion) of the sentence; e.g. School starts **at** 8.00 am. *They are usually followed by a noun or gerund. (~ing word)* I am good **at** <u>running</u>.

*'***to***' is not often followed by a gerund; there are exceptions.***

Some prepositions are 'wedded' to verbs or adjectives; e.g, **'look at', '**listen **to', 'good at', 'interested in',** *etc.*

They can change the meaning of the verbs, as in the case of phrasal verbs. For instance; **get** *does not have the same meaning as* **get up**.

Some prepositions may be put before **relative** *pronouns or at the end of their clauses.*

***exceptions**: I'm looking forward to} meeting/seeing/going/playing/travelling, etc.
I'm used to} eating/talking/visiting, etc.

Note: *Some of these words can be used as prefixes and have far more uses than I indicate here; the intention is to provide the most common ones.*

Now let's look at some of the more common prepositions. Here I need to add that in some instances adverbs also double as prepositions; words such as, **after** *and* **before**. *They can also be conjunctions.* ***This is why I think grammar should be taught by position of words rather than explanation.***

about

functions	examples
Indicates content of books, movies, topics, etc.	What was the movie **about**? He's going to talk **about** movies.
Indicates approximation of time, numbers, money and place.	Can you come **about** 2.00 pm? There were **about** 25 people in the room. I have **about** $4.00. It happened **about** here.

above

functions	examples
Indicates a higher position with no contact or movement.	The eyebrows are **above** the eyes.
A separation, not touching. A clear distance.	There were clouds **above** the mountains. The basketball team were all well **above** 2 metres tall.
Can begin a sentence.	**Above** the garage, there's a bedroom.

after

functions	examples
Indicates the reverse of **before**.	The children came home **after** we had gone to bed.
Indicates a following.	The police went **after** the robbers.
Can begin a sentence.	**After** dinner, we went for a walk.
Generally not used for physical positions.	~~Park the car **after** the tree.~~

against

functions	examples
Indicates disagreement or opposition.	He was **against** the idea and refused to support it.
Touch.	The police pushed **against** the crowd. He leaned the ladder **against** the wall.
Indicates a backdrop.	The mountain looked magnificent **against** the blue sky.

along

functions	examples
Moving parallel to; side by side.	We walked **along** the beach.
Accompany; together.	Would you like to come **along** with us?

among

functions	examples
Within three or more things or persons.	**Among** my students there is one from Mongolia.
Within a group.	
Mingling.	Who **among** you is a doctor?
Can begin a sentence.	She walked **among** the guests. **Among** my books, I have several mystery novels.
Not used with uncountable nouns.	~~There was an ant **among** the sugar.~~

around/round

functions	examples
Generally the same functions as **about**; also connotes **more or less**; except for content or topic. Avoiding the main or essential topic. In various places.	Can you come **around** 2.00 pm? There were **around** 25 people in the room I have **around** $4.00. It happened **around** here. ~~This book is **around** India.~~ He just talked **around** the topic. The children ran **around** the room.

as

functions	examples
Indicates that someone or something is being used in a way different from its original purpose. Introducing a reason. Being employed in a particular way.	I didn't have a ruler so I used a book **as** a ruler. Don't use that knife **as** a screwdriver! **As** it was raining, we decided to stay home. He works **as** a waiter.

at

functions	examples
Indicates preciseness in time and place, particularly large public places. Shows an exactness. Joins adjectives to nouns to show a degree of skill. Shows a rate of cost or speed. Used with some superlatives. With night.	They arrived **at** 6.00pm. I'll meet you **at** the restaurant. They were looking **at** us. He's very good **at** maths. Potatoes are **at** $2.00 a kg. He drove **at** 120 kph. **At** his best, he is unbeatable. **At** least we got there in time. Most of us sleep **at** night.

away

functions	examples
Not here, gone for a reasonably long time. A separation. Distance Has an emphatic use.	He is **away** for the moment. Peter has gone **away.** How far **away** is the theatre? Go **away**!

before

functions	examples
Indicates a position in time, an occurrence preceding another. Not generally used for physical positions, but there are exceptions. Can have a metaphorical meaning.	The students came in **before** the teacher. I brush my teeth **before** I go to bed. Be home **before** 11.00 pm. They rolled out the red carpet **before** the king. The police placed the evidence **before** the judge.

behind

functions	examples
Indicates a position to the rear of another position. Indicates an inability to keep up with a schedule. To follow; be a little slower.	The garden is **behind** the house. He is **behind** in his payments. I need to stay on at work, I am falling **behind** in my work. The little girl ran **behind** her parents.

below

functions	examples
Functions almost the reverse of **above**. No contact with the higher position. Indicates no movement.	The eyes are **below** the eyebrows. The ball hit him just **below** the elbow. Peter got **below** the pass mark in his exam.

between

functions	examples
Within two things or groups of things or persons. Just two things or persons. Sharing a secret. Can start a sentence.	He sat **between** his sisters. *(Two sisters)* I can't choose **between** these two teams. They put a fence **between** the two houses. **Between** you and I, I think he's mistaken.

beyond

functions	examples
Indicates a cut off point in time and space. Past a certain point.	I cannot stay out **beyond** 11.00 pm. We are not permitted to go **beyond** the gates. Nobody is allowed **beyond** the barrier. The village is **beyond** the hills. Very few people live **beyond** a 100. Quantum Theory is **beyond** my understanding.

by

functions	examples
Indicates moving past a fixed point.	He went **by** the post office.
Next to.	Sit **by** me.
Completion time.	I have to finish my work **by** 5.00 pm.
Using a conveyance or other means.	I came here **by** bus.
Used in passive sentences.	The mountains are covered **by** snow.

down

functions	examples
Indicates going towards the ground.	They went **down** the stairs.
Indicates a position.	They met **down** at the pub.
Not functioning.	The copier is **down**; we're waiting for the technician.
Feeling depressed (sad).	You look really **down**, what's the matter?

during

functions	examples
Indicates a length of time within which something happens. The time is indicated by reference rather than actual time. Has the same connotation as **while**; however, **during** is followed by a noun phrase rather than a sentence.	I was born **during** World War II. (World War II was about 5 years long) The farmers rest **during** the hot part of the day. Please don't smoke **during** the meal.

for

functions	examples
Indicates purpose (use).	A chair is **for** sitting on.
Amount of money or time.	I bought this chair **for** $10.00. I waited **for** 10 minutes.
In place of someone or something.	I'm writing this letter **for** Peter, he's hurt his hand.
Directed towards someone or something.	I bought these flowers **for** you. I'm going to the shop **for** some flowers.

from

functions	examples
Indicates a separation.	I bought this book **from** that shop.
A starting point.	The classes are **from** the 3rd of January.
An origin.	He comes **from** Spain.

in

functions	examples
Indicates non-movement.	My pen is **in** my pocket.
Contained in a particular situation.	I watched **in** horror.
	They are living **in** luxury.
Confined in small enclosed spaces.	The car is **in** the garage.
Within a long period of time: month, decade, year, century.	**in** May, **in** the 1930s, **in** 2005, **in** the 21st century.
Part of day.	**in** the morning/afternoon/ evening.
Adjective+subject/topic.	(~~in the night~~) interested **in** football/
With languages.	Literature.
To be early for an event.	Can you write it **in** English?
	We were **in** time for the train.

inside

functions	examples
Indicates being confined in an enclosed space.	When it began to rain, everyone went **inside**.
	I found a $5.00 note **inside** the book.
	No one was **inside** the building.
Within a time.	She finished **inside** 4 minutes.

in front of

functions	examples
Indicates a physical position preceding another position; can be stationary or moving.	Park the car **in front of** the red one. He walked **in front of** me.
	The garden was **in front of** the house.

Near/close to/next to

functions	examples
Near/close to indicate in the vicinity of. **Next to** indicates a side by side position.	The church is **near/ close to** the railway station. The church is **next to** the railway station. *(side by side; facing in the same direction)*

of (/ov/)

functions	examples
Indicates a belonging to. A relationship.	The colour **of** my shirt is red. The boyfriend **of** my daughter is an artist.
A togetherness.	All **of** the pictures were interesting.
Dates. Not used with proper nouns.	Today is the 4th **of** April. ~~The leg **of** Peter is broken.~~

Off (/of/)

functions	examples
Indicates a separation. Indicates a departure, a going away from. A disconnection. Going rotten. Losing interest in something or someone.	He took **off** his shirt. He went **off** yesterday. Please turn **off** the radio. The milk is **off**. I've gone **off** TV. Mary has gone **off** Peter.
Completely.	We have finished **off** all the milk.

on

functions	examples
Indicates contact, touch, connection.	Put the picture **on** the wall. The book is **on** the table. Turn **on** the radio.
Used with most words with **'day'*** in them. Dates. Used with media. Used with words such as, rely, depend, etc. Used with large transport. Used with 'open' forms of transport. Indicates a continuation. With an expected time.	I came here **on** Monday. My birthday is **on** the 30th of December. I heard it **on** the radio./I saw it **on** TV. I can rely/depend **on** you. I like travelling **on** buses/planes/ships. I like riding **on** a cart/bike/horse. He just keeps **on** talking. The train left **on** time.
***yesterday**, **today** and **tomorrow** have no prepositions before them.	
Both **on** and **in** can be used to indicate movement by joining them to **to**; for instance; **onto** and **into**. **Examples:** The cat climbed **onto** the roof./She walked **into** the room.	

opposite

functions	examples
Facing each other. Totally different. Sharing a part in a play or movie.	Peter sat **opposite** Mary. Black is the **opposite** of white. Mary played **opposite** Peter in the play.

out

functions	examples
Indicates a separation. A departure. Not have; use up. Appear, become visible. To reveal one's sexual orientation.	He is **out**. I'm going **out** tonight. He went **out** a few minutes ago. I'm **out** of money. We are **out** of milk. The book hasn't come **out** yet. Peter came **out** at he Gay Parade.

outside

functions	examples
Indicates not being confined. Being beyond a limit. The outer part.	The children were asked to play **outside**. Mathematics is **outside** my area of expertise. Entering the building was **outside** the jurisdiction of the police. The **outside** of the car was very clean.

over

functions	examples
Indicates movement, similar to above. Indicates distance. To be at a higher position. Covering or touching. Complete, end. To review or study, teach.	The birds flew **over** the trees. The railway station is **over** there. The temperature was **over** 30˚. The police put a sheet **over** the body. The movie will be **over** soon. The teacher went **over** the lesson.

since

functions	examples
Indicates the beginning time of an action; most frequently used with the present perfect and present perfect continuous tenses. Indicates that the duration of the action has not ended. It is also a conjunction. Also indicates reason.	They have lived in the same house **since** they came to New Zealand. They have lived here **since** 1980. I have been waiting for the bus **since** 10.00 am. They have been playing in the park **since** 2.00 pm. He left early **since** he wasn't feeling well.

to

functions	examples
Indicates movement to a precise destination, hence it is not used with words that do not indicate an exact destination; such as **home, downtown, here, there, shopping,** etc.	We are walking **to** the park. I am going ~~to home~~.
It joins two verbs as in semi-modals.	I want **to** buy that car.
It joins adjectives to verbs.	I was very happy **to** see you.
It is also used to show purpose or reason.	I came to NZ **to** learn English.
It is usually followed by base verbs.	I like **to** play football.
Not normally followed by gerunds.	~~I like to playing football.~~
However, there are exceptions.	look forward **to** seeing/meeting ... be-verb+used **to** playing/walking ...

towards

functions	examples
Indicates movement to a particular, *but not exact*, destination /in the direction of.	They walked **towards** the north. They walked **towards** the church. *(not to the church)*.
Indicates having a goal in mind. Indicates a tendency.	We are saving **towards** buying a house. He leans **towards** a more liberal attitude. We began to feel peckish **towards** noon.
Indicates a position in time and space.	The book was a little frayed **towards** the edges.
In North America the **s** is deleted: **toward**	

through

functions	examples
From one side to the other.	We walked **through** the park. Look **through** the window.
From beginning to end. Complete, not need any more.	The teacher went **through** the lesson. I'm **through** with this book. She is **through** with him.
Successful.	They all got **through** their exams. He came **through** an illness.

under

functions	examples
In a lower position but within the confines of the higher object.	The shoes were **under** the bed. They went for a walk **under** the bridge. The meal was well **under** $50.00.
There is a possibility of contact.	I found my pen **under** my bag.
Beneath and underneath functions in almost the same way as **under**. We sat **beneath** the stars. It was getting cold so we all got **underneath** the blankets.	

until/till

functions	examples
Indicates a point in time (or place) when a change takes place. The action is disrupted or changed.	I waited for her **until/till** 9.00 pm. He drank **until/till** the bottle was empty. She wasn't satisfied **until/till** she got a full refund. Stay on the train **until/till** you get to Wellington.

up

functions	examples
Indicates to raise or increase.	Prices are going **up** again. When he saw the police he shouldn't have sped **up.**
To lift your face towards the sky. To finish or complete.	The children are all grown **up**. They looked **up** at the low flying airplane. Drink **up** your milk. I used **up** all my money. Tie **up** your shoelaces.
To get out of bed/wake up	I'm **up** around 6.00 am.

with

functions	examples
Indicates three things together.	She came to school **with** her bag. He came down **with** the flu.
Accompany. Belong to. Can start a sentence.	He went to Africa **with** his family. He is **with** the Labour Party. *(A member of)* **With** this ring, I thee wed.
without: absence of; not have. She came to school **without** her bag. His family left **without** him. **within:** being inside a defined time or space. He will be here **within** 5 minutes. Everything must fit **within** this space.	

PRONOUNS

Pronouns perform various functions; as can be seen by the chart. Some replace proper and common (concrete) nouns **(subject and object)***; thus relieving us from having to constantly repeat the same words over and over again; others show ownership* **(adjectival, possessive)***; emphasis or subject/ object sameness* **(reflexive)***, and information* **(relative).**

Pronouns are:

subject*	object	adjectival	reflexive	possessive	relative***
I	me	my	myself	mine	who
You**	you	your	yourself(ves)	yours	that
He	him	his	himself	his	which
She	her	her	herself	hers	who(m)
It	it	its	itself	its	whose
They	them	their	themselves	theirs	where
We	us	our	ourselves	ours	when
					why

Note: **Subject pronouns usually have a capital letter, unless used in the question form.*
** 'You' is both a singular and a plural word, depending on how it is used. It is replacing 'one' when used to refer to anyone or everyone. Look at the sentences below.
***The relative pronouns do not coincide with the other pronouns alongside them.

You are a very lucky person. *(one person)*
You must all give me your homework tomorrow. *(more than one person)*
One ought not to smoke *is being replaced by* **You** ought not to smoke.

Subject *pronouns replace the* **subject** *in the initial sentence in subsequent sentences. Look at these sentence.*

Peter is a teacher. **He** is 23 years old. **He** has been teaching for three years.

Object *pronouns replace the* **object** *in the initial sentence in subsequent sentences. Look at these sentence.*

I bought **a beautiful book**. I bought **it** in Hamilton. I paid $250.00 for **it**.

Adjectival *pronouns are always placed before the word which requires ownership. Look at these sentences.*

This is **my** book,
Our house is quite small.
Can you look after **her** bag?

Possessive *pronouns can be both* **subject** *or* **object** *of the sentence. They always stand alone, unlike the* **adjectival** *pronouns. Look at these sentences.*

My book is red, **yours** is blue.
My book is red, what colour is **yours**?
Theirs has a pink top.

Reflexive *pronouns can be put in various positions in the sentence, which can change the concept of the sentence somewhat. Look at these sentences.*

I **myself** saw the accident. *(emphatic use)*
I saw the accident **myself**. *(change (lessening) of emphasis)*
You **yourself** told me this. *(emphatic use and the object of the verb 'told' is different).*
You told **yourself** this.

Relative *pronouns are a sort of connector; they replace the pronoun in the second, informative, sentence forming one sentence.*

Here are the relative pronouns and what they relate to.

Pronoun	relates to
who	subject persons, [boy(s), girls(s)], etc., and proper nouns, (Peter, Mary, Ali) etc.
that	things, [chairs(s), table(s)], etc., and other living things, [cat(s), dog(s)], etc.
which	the same things as 'that' but there is a subtle difference.
who(m)	object person(s) and proper nouns.
whose	persons, things and living things; usually followed by a noun.
what	relates to the action preceding it.
when	time phrases and usually follows them. Not a relative pronoun in the true sense.
where	a place.
why	a reason and usually follows the word 'reason'. But may be omitted.

WHO and WHOM

Who *is used to define or give extra information about people located in the subject portion of the sentence.*

Whom *is used to define or give information about people located in the object (completion) portion of the sentence. It is becoming common practice to drop the* **m** *in* **whom** *in spoken English.* *Look at this sentence.*

The boy **who** lives next door has invited Peter, **who (m)** he only met yesterday, to his party.

THAT or WHICH

That *can refer to both people and things,* **which** *cannot refer to people. For instance,* 'the man **that** I saw'; 'the book **that** I bought'; 'the book **which** I bought' *are correct; whereas,* 'the man **which** I saw' *is not.*

That *also follows words such as;* 'much' *and* 'all'. *E.g.* 'There is much **that** I like about Auckland.' 'This book is all **that** I need.'

It is preferable to use **which** *with non-defining clauses. Look at these sentences.*

Auckland, **which** has the sea to its east and west, can only expand to the north and south. This is the book, **which** I saw in the shop. *(The book is identified by 'This')*

It can also suggest a choice. Look at these sentences.

The book **which** I bought was quite expensive.
The restaurant **which** we went to had delicious Thai food.

Which *can also refer to the whole sentence preceding it. Look at these sentences.*

He always comes late to class, **which** upsets the teacher.
He is always cracking his knuckles, **which** is really annoying.
In the summer the weather is moderate, **which** makes for a good holiday.

WHOSE

Whose *shows ownership and replaces the possessive pronoun in the second, informative sentence. Look at these sentences.*

This is Peter. **His** house is next to mine. This is Peter, **whose** house is next to mine.

WHAT

What *can be used as a relative pronoun if it is not preceded by a noun. Look at these sentences:*

'You can have the money (**that**) I promised you.' (**that** *can be omitted)*
'You can have the money **what** I promised you.' *X*

In the first sentence **that** *refers to* '**the money**'; *in the second sentence* **what** *is* '**the money**' *itself; hence* '**the money**' *is redundant; the sentence should read;*

'You can have **what** I promised you.'
'I can't understand **what** she sees in him.'

It can also be used with adjectives such as funny, etc. Look at these sentences.

It's funny **what** people do if they don't think they are being observed. It's amazing **what** people say out of ignorance.

When, where, why *don't really need a noun to precede it when the noun is redundant to the situation. Look at these sentences.*

This is the time **when** *I leave.*
This is **when** I leave.
This is the room **where** *I keep my books.*
This is **where** I keep my books.
We don't know the reason **why** *he resigned.*
We don't know **why** he resigned.

Why *can also be used after words such as 'certain', 'understand','explain', etc. Look at these sentences.*

It isn't clear **why** he left so suddenly.
We aren't sure **why** we were refused visas.
He didn't explain **why** she refused his offer.

*Let's look at how the **relative** pronoun replaces the subject or object **pronoun**.*

*The boy lives next door. **He** is a student.*
The boy **who** is a student lives next door.
The boy **who** lives next door is a student.
*This is my friend Jane. I have known **her** since we were teenagers.*
This is my friend Jane, **who (m)** I have known since we were teenagers.
*I was talking to a man at the party. **It** was two weeks ago.*
I was talking to a man at a party (**that** was) two weeks ago.
*She finally bought the painting. She had always wanted **it**.*
<u>She</u> finally bought the painting (**that/which**) <u>she</u> had always wanted. *
*They told us a story. We found **it** very interesting.*
<u>They</u> told us a story, (**which/that**) <u>we</u> found very interesting. *
We found **what** they told us very interesting.**
What they told us, we found very interesting.**
*Have you met Peter? I bought **his** house.*
Have you met Peter, **whose** house I bought?
Is there any reason **why you won't do it**?
Could you give a reason **why you wouldn't buy this house**?

*When the sentence has two subjects the relative pronoun may be omitted.
**In these two sentences there are no clear objects so the relative pronoun cannot be omitted.

PUNCTUATION

Comma (,) =
1. *lists, series:* I visited Spain, France, Portugal, etc.
2. *adjectives:* He was a tall, dark, mysterious man.
3. *when conjunctions start sentences:* If I knew you were coming, I'd've baked a cake.
4. *non-defining relative clauses, extra information:* Pierre, who teaches in room 10, is from France.
5. *adverbs:* John, surprisingly, is a good tennis player.
6. *numbers:* 3,000; 300,000; 3,000,000.
7. *before conjunction in long sentences:* I decided to stay home, but Mary chose to go to the cinema.

Colon (:) =
1. *before an explanation:* We decided not to drive to the coast: the weather had changed for the worse.
2. *in theatre scripts:* JOHN: And how are you today, my dear?

   MARY: Terrible. My dear, terrible.
3. *begin lists:* The fruit grown in India are: bananas, pears, apples, mangoes, etc.
4. *subtitles:* Anthropology: the study of humans.

Semi-colon (;) =
1. *instead of a full stop; especially with closely related sentences:* It's a lovely morning; let's hope it stays that way.
2. *List with long sentences:* First, I'm thinking of going to the supermarket; then perhaps, I'll go to the gym; or maybe I'll stop off at a cafe and have a cup of coffee.

Full stop (.) =
1. *separates two sentences, two ideas:* They went to Africa last year. They went by ship.
2. *ends a sentence:* They left yesterday.
3. *acronyms:* U.S.A. (not in common use these days)

4. *decimal points:* 1.5; 2.75; 0.25.

5. *dates:*30.12.1940.

6. *time:* 11.45 am, 12.00 noon.

Exclamation Mark (!) =

1. *expresses surprise, anger, fear:* Really! How dare you!

   A shout: Helloo!

Interrobang (!?/?!) =

1. *indicates surprise, astonishment, bewilderment, etc:* He fell down a well?!

   Him!?

Question mark (?) =

1. *expresses a query or asks a questions:* You are a teacher? Are you a teacher?

   Where do you live?

Quotation marks ("___") /('___') =

1. *double quotation marks are used to indicate direct speech within a narrative*: "You can't come in here."

2. *single quotation marks are used to insert quotations taken from another source:* Jonathan who was referred to as 'the star of the show' gave a brilliant performance.

3. *single quotation marks are also used to insert word(s) that are not a part of the sentence but are being referred to:* The words 'that' and 'what' are not interchangeable in all cases.

Charles Dickens used "----" to incase dialogue in his novels.

Apostrophe (') =

1. *to show a word's been shortened:* n't; I'd've.

2. *to show possession:* Ferooz's class is in room 10.

3. *used before 's' in singular words and after 's' in plural words to show possession:* the boy's book; the boys' book.

Dash (-) =
1. *a dash has space on either side.* **(-)**
2. *can be used in the same way as colons, semi-colons or brackets:* I'm interested – if the price is right. She – a teacher – loved children.

Hyphen (-) =
1. *a hyphen has no space on either side.* *(-)*
2. *joins some compound words:* box-office: ticket-office.
3. *two part adjectives:* blue-eyed; nice-looking.
4. *phrases as adjectives:* out-of-work person; shoot-to-kill policy.

Brackets or Parentheses () =
1. *can be used in the same way as a dash or comma for the inclusion of extra information:* She **(**a teacher**)** loved children. Patricia **(**16**)** was declared the winner.

Capital letter =
1. *All new sentences begin with a capital letter:* **The** boys are playing football.
2. *The first letter after a full stop, exclamation or question mark is a capital letter:* **The** boys are playing football. **They** always play on Wednesdays.
3. *All specific names start with a capital letter; proper nouns, books and movie titles, titles in general, names of cities and countries, acronyms, days, months, etc:* **Peter, The History of India, Gone with the Wind, Sir/Madam, Auckland, New Zealand, U.S.A, U.K, Monday, January.**

APOSTROPHE

Used to show possession with:
1. *'living' common nouns.*
2. *proper nouns.*
3. *cities & countries.*
4. *but not usually with inanimate things (lifeless).*

–'s = single possessive.

This is used to show that something belongs to one person or thing: This is the boy**'s** book. *(This book belongs to **one** boy,)* I haven't heard today**'s** news. *(I haven't heard the news for today.)*
It is also used to indicate an occurrence within a given time in the future: I am leaving New Zealand in two week**'s** time. The judge will give her verdict in five day**s'*** time.

There is some disagreement over the use of **'s or **s'**; take your pick.*

– s' = plural possessive.
This is used to show that something belongs to more than one person or thing: This is the boys**'** football. *(The football belongs to **two or more** boys.)* These teams**'** uniforms are very similar. *(There are several teams that have similar uniforms.)*

s' or s's with words or names ending with 's'.
This is used when words naturally end with an 's', often proper nouns: These are Darius**'** shoes or These are Darius**'s** shoes, The Jones**'** children are very polite or The Jones**'s** children are very polite. *(I prefer to use the first alternative.) The pronunciation is the same for both uses.*

Abbreviations.
Sometimes we don't (see?) need to use all the letters in a word, usually when we are speaking or want to show that someone is speaking when we write.

      'i' *in* is = He's
      'i' *in* is = It's **(its** *is a possessive pronoun)*
      'a' *in* I am = I'm
      'a' *in* are = They're
      'ha' *in* have = I've got
      'ha' *in* has = She's gone
      'o' *in* not = They aren't
      'ha' *in* had = I'd
      'coul' *in* could = I'd
      'woul' *in* would = I'd
      'woul' 'ha' *in* I would have = I'd've
      'wi' *in* will = I'll

*Punctuations can be more complex than this straight-forward explanation. And what do we make of **won't**? Look up its history. Or **shan't**, for that matter! **The misuse of the apostrophe is ubiquitous!***

TENSES*

Tenses indicate the time of the action depicted in the sentence. Tenses can be single words like **play** *or* **plays***; or a combination of words like* **am going to buy***. This part of the sentence is usually placed between the* **subject** *and* **completion** *of the sentence. When* **modals** *or* **semi- modals** *are used they become a part of the tense.*

Here are some examples of the various tenses in the active form.

tenses	form
present simple	am, is, are; play, plays, go, goes, etc.
past simple	was, were; played, went, etc.
present continuous	am playing, is going, are playing, etc.
past continuous	was playing, was going, etc. (with other **past** sentences)
present perfect	have played, has played, have gone, has gone, etc.
past perfect	had played, had gone, etc.
pp continuous	have been playing, has been going, etc.
ptp continuous	had been playing, had been going, etc.
future	prs, ppc, some modals, some semi-modals plus **future time**.

Now here are some examples of the various tenses in the passive form.

tenses	form
present simple	**am/is/are** played; **am/is/are** taken, etc.
past simple	**was/were** played; **was/were** taken, etc.
present continuous	**am/is/are being** played; **am/is/are being** taken, etc.
past continuous	**was/were being** played; **was/were being** taken, etc.
present perfect	**have been** played; **has been** taken, etc.
past perfect	**had been** played; **had been** taken, etc.
pp continuous**	**have been being** played; **has been being** taken, etc.
pt p continuous**	**had been being** played; **had been being** taken. etc
future	**will** be/**is going to** be/**will have** been played plus **future time**.
**These passive forms are not frequently used.	

*Note: *I am using the term* **tense** *to include the term* **aspect**. **For a brief explanation see page 28.**

Keep in mind that any word that is **not** *an* **auxiliary** *verb (be-verbs, do, have, modals and semi- modals) is a* **main** *verb.*

PRESENT SIMPLE active

The present simple is used when we want to express an unchanging condition, or at least for a long time, or when we know that something is true, even for the moment.

There are two types of verbs that are used to indicate the present simple:

Present simple be-verbs; **am, is, are**.
Present simple main verbs; **play(s), go(es)**, *etc.*

The present simple is used in situations which show **facts (things that don't or can't change), habits/customs,** *and* **programmes/routines/ timetables**.
It is also used to show a programmed (routine) **future** *action.*
The auxiliary verbs for the present simple main verb are **do** *and* **does**.

Here are some **facts**.

The sky **is** blue. The sky **isn't** green.
Water **is** wet.
Two hydrogen molecules and one oxygen molecule **make** water.
Two plus two **is** four. Two plus two **isn't** five.
He **teaches** English as a second language. He **doesn't teach** German.

Here are some **habits** *people or other living things might have.*

She **smokes**. I **don't smoke**.
The Chinese mainly **drink** tea. In the U.S. they mainly **drink** coffee.
My cat **sleeps** under the sofa.
My dog **doesn't eat** fish.

Here are some **programmes/routines/timetables**.

I **leave** my house every morning at 8.00 am.
My favourite TV programme **starts** at 8.30 pm.
I **brush** my teeth before I **have** breakfast.
The train **leaves** tomorrow at 9.30 am. *(routine future)*

Present simple Be-verb and Main verb.
Be-verbs

The **be-verb** *is the only verb in the English language that can stand alone in the positive, negative and question forms; look at these sentences:*

I **am** a teacher.	**Am** I a teacher?	I **am** not a teacher.
Mary **is** my teacher.	**Is** Mary your teacher?	Mary **isn't** my teacher.

Main verbs

The other auxiliary verbs don't function in a similar manner.

She **has*** a brother.	**Has** she a brother?	She **has** not a brother.
She **does*** the cooking.	**Does** she the cooking?	She **does** not the cooking.

Does *she have a brother? She* **doesn't** *have a brother.*

***While this is permissible the question and negative forms are not in common use any longer. They become:**

The present simple also experiences other changes, depending on what type of subject is used.

Subjects **I, You, They** *and* **plural words** *do not affect the verb which remains in its base form.*

I/You/They/The **boys play** football.

However, subjects that are **singular** *or* **uncountable** *require the suffixes* **'s'** *or* **'es'** *be added to the verb.*

The **boy** plays football/The **rain** falls in autumn.

The suffix **'es'** *is usually used with verbs and words that end in* **'ch', 'o', 'sh', 'ss', 'x',** *and* **'zz'***; zeroes, churches, classes, watches, and so on ...* **'s'** *is added to most other verbs.*

When using adverbs of frequency, they are usually put **after** *the* **be-verb** *and* **before** *the verb.*

He is **often** late.

They are **seldom** seen here.

The class **always** starts at 8.00 am.

I **usually** go to bed at midnight.

Question and negative.

Both forms of sentences must use the auxiliary verb **do/does** *when the sentence contains a* **main**
verb. For instance:

I **play** tennis.	**Do** you play tennis?	I **don't play** tennis.
He **plays** tennis.	**Does** he **play*** tennis?	He **doesn't play*** tennis.
The class **starts** at 8.00 am.	**Does** the class **start** at 8.00 am.	The class **doesn't start** at 8.00 am.

***Note:** when the auxiliary verb* **'do'** *is used with the 3rd person; the* **'s'** *of the main verb is transferred to the* **'do'** *and the main verb loses its* **'s'**.

Present (always) time indicators.

statement	time indicator	duration
I go for a run We go to the cinema Mary goes to the hair salon etc.	every	day. morning. afternoon. Saturday. etc.

statement	time indicator (frequency)	duration
I go for a run We go to the cinema Mary goes to the hair salon etc.	**once/twice**/etc, **a two/ three/four**/etc, **times a every other every second/third**/etc,	week. day. month. etc.

*Duration words which end with ~***ly** *can be put at the end of the sentence (adverb) or put before a noun (adjective). Interesting eh? Look at these sentences.*

My mail is delivered **daily**.

The Metro is a **monthly** magazine.

I do my shopping **weekly**.

We have **fortnightly** meetings at my place of work.

And then we have days of the week, which are usually preceded by the preposition **on.** *Look at these sentences.*

My children go to dancing lessons on **Saturdays.**
We do our grocery shopping on **Fridays.**
We usually go to the cinema on **Tuesdays.**

The **present simple** *with a* **future time indicator** *can express an action in the future. Look at these sentences.*

statement	future time indicator
I leave for France She goes to the gym The film starts etc.	**tonight**. **next** week. **on** Monday. **this** evening. etc.

There is another feature of the present simple which is called the **dramatic present.** *The retelling of book or movie plots (since they never change) can be done in the present simple to give them immediacy and hence heighten the suspense. It is also a very good device for maintaining attention when telling personal anecdotes! Look at this.*

Event in the **past tense***:*

I was walking home from the cinema and suddenly I felt disorientated, but not only that; I also felt I was being followed. I stopped to listen, but I was met with silence.

Same event in the **dramatic present***:*

I am walking home from the cinema, and suddenly I feel disorientated, but not only that; I also feel I'm being followed. I stop to listen, but I am met with silence.

The first version distances both the narrator and listener from the event being related. The story in the dramatic present draws the narrator and listener into the atmosphere of the event. **Try it!**

PRESENT SIMPLE passive

The present simple passive is made by combining the **present simple be-verb** *and the* **3rd/past participle** *(regular and irregular verbs). The present simple be-verb indicates that the action is a regular action occurring several times. The sentences look like this:.*

object	verb	3rd/past participle	by subject (completion)
1st person = I	**am**	taken	to school by bus.
		taught	to be polite.
		chased	in New Zealand.
		made	in Japan.
3rd person = He, She,	**is**	sold	all over the world.
It **singular** = The dog,		bought	in Muslim countries.
My car, Peter, etc.		walked	in cool cellars.
uncountables = Cheese,		grown	to the zoo.
Petroleum, etc.		played	by dogs.
		shown	from left to right.
		read	to the park after school.
2nd person = You	**are**	drunk	in the Middle-East.
plurals = Apples, Cars,		produced	by visitors.
The children, They, etc.		stolen	in the market place.
		given	by my parents.
		asked	etc.
		etc.	

Now let's combine some of these four segments into sentences.

I **am taught** by my parents.
These children **are taught** by their parents.
Cheese **is sold** in the market place.
Apples **are grown** in New Zealand.
Toyotas **are made** in Japan.
Football **is played** all over the world.
You **are drunk** in the marketplace. *(You are not a liquid! – a bit ambiguous!)*
This question **is** often **asked** by visitors.
The zebra **is sold** to the zoo. *(Not likely to be a recurring event)*
Petroleum **is produced** in the Middle-East.

PAST SIMPLE active

The past simple expresses a fact in the past which might or might not be true any longer. These sentences are always accompanied by a definite **past time***; either in the statement itself or within the discourse.*

The verb is formed in two ways; by adding the suffix 'ed' or using a new verb, the **irregular** *verbs. There are some verbs (irregular) that do not change, '***cut***', for instance.*

*The auxiliary verbs change into new verbs; '***am***' and '***is***' become '***was***'; '***are***' becomes '***were***'; '***do***' and '***does***' become '***did***'; '***have***' and '***has***' become '***had***'. Hence they are part of the irregular verbs.*

Negative *and* **question** *sentences use the past simple auxiliary verbs. Look at these sentences.*

Jonathan **was** born in 1940.
A fact in the past and true for always.

Jonathan **lived** in Spain before he came to New Zealand.
A fact in the past which is no longer true as he lives in New Zealand now. Note that each sentence has a time reference. As does the discourse below.

Where **were** you in **2005**?
I **was** in High school.
Was she happy in Spain? *(she is not in Spain now)*
Did you enjoy the party? *(the party is over)*
He **did**n't arrive on time. *(he was late)*

When using **did** *in the* **negative** *and* **question** *form, the main verb is always in the* **base** *form.*

Did you **play** tennis yesterday afternoon?
What **did** you **do** yesterday afternoon?
I **did**n't **do** anything.

Past time indicators are often put at the end of the sentence, but may also begin the sentence, in which case, it can be followed by a comma.

Past time indicators.

statement	time indicator
I didn't come to school There were two major wars They bought their house etc.	**yesterday.** **in the 20th century.** **the other day.** etc.

statement	number	duration	time indicator
I saw that movie I met her They played that team etc.	a a few one two three four etc.	second(s) moment(s) hour(s) day(s) week(s) month(s) etc.	**ago.**

statement	time indicator	time of day
I saw that movie I met her They played that team etc.	**yesterday**	morning. afternoon. evening. etc.

statement	time indicator	duration
I saw that movie I met her They played that team etc.	**last**	night. week. month. year. decade. etc.

statement	time indicator	statement
I saw that movie I met her They played that team etc.	**after** **before** **when** **while**	I came to New Zealand. I met you. they were in Spain. I was coming on the plane. etc.

statement	time indicator	time
I went home I met her They played that team etc.	**after** **before**	midnight. 3.00 pm. lunch. etc.

Here are some sentences putting the segments together.

They left for New York **yesterday**.
They left for New York in **2007**.
They left for New York a few months **ago**.

They left for New York **yesterday** morning.
They left for New York **last** night.
They left for New York **after** they got married.

Adverbs of frequency may also be used in past simple sentences.

PAST SIMPLE passive.

The past simple passive is made by combining the **past simple be-verb** *and the* **3ʳᵈ/past participle** *(regular and irregular verbs). The past simple be-verb indicates that the action is a one-off. It talks about specific objects which have been acted on in a given past. The particular act is not to be repeated. In these sentences the* **object** *may need to be defined with the use of determiners; such as: articles, possessive adjectives, demonstrative adjective/pronouns, etc. The sentences look like this:*

object	verb	3ʳᵈ/past participle	subject (completion)
1ˢᵗ person = I **3ʳᵈ person** = He, She, It **singular** = The dog, My car, Peter, etc **uncountables** = Cheese, Petroleum, etc.	**was**	taken taught chased made sold walked grown played shown	to school by bus. to be polite. in New Zealand. in Japan. all over the world. in Muslim countries. to the zoo. by the cat. to the park after school.
2ⁿᵈ person = You **plurals** = The apples, These cars, Her children, They, etc.	**were**	drunk stolen given asked etc.	in the Middle-East. a lot of questions. in the market place. from the Art Gallery. etc.

Now let's combine some of these four segments into sentences.

I **was taken** to school by bus last week.
My watch **was made** in Switzerland.
The milk **was drunk** by the cat this morning.
These apples **were grown** in New Zealand.
Several paintings **were stolen** from the Art Gallery.
He **was asked** a lot of questions
This book **was read** all over the world.

PRESENT CONTINUOUS active

The present continuous sentence is formed by the combining of three units; a **be-verb***; a* **main- verb** *plus ~***ing***.*

Whatever action that can be **seen** *or* **heard** ***at the moment*** *can be expressed in the present continuous form. The contrast with the present simple is that while the present simple implies permanency, the present continuous is a prolonged action which is expected to come to an end at some point; i.e. it implies* **change***. So when I say, 'I* **wear** *glasses.' I am stating that the glasses are a permanent feature of my dressing. And when I say, 'I am* **wearing** *a red shirt.' I am indicating that at some future point I might be wearing a shirt of a different colour.*

In the present continuous we use three be-verbs, **am** *(with* **'I'***),* **are** *(with* **2ⁿᵈ person** *and* **plurals***), and is* *(with* **3ʳᵈ person, singular** *and* **uncountables nouns***).*

*The main verb, in general, is not affected by the adding of the suffix ~***ing***, so* **play** *becomes* **playing***;* **go - going***; etc. However, there are verbs that require a repetition of the last letter;* **ban - banning***:* **hop - hopping***, etc. The general rule is: words with* **short vowels** *sounds* **repeat** *the last letter; words with* **long vowel** *sounds* **don't***; e.g.* **hop - hopping***;* **hope - hoping***.*

See TWO Ts OR NOT TWO Ts on page 178.

This chart separates the uses of the be-verbs.

subject (1st person)	be-verb	main verb	completion
I	am	playing brushing walking to thinking of etc.	tennis. my teeth. school. buying a car. etc.
subject (2nd person, plurals, etc)	**be-verb**	**main verb**	**completion**
You The boys These people Those girls etc.	are	sitting running waiting dancing etc.	in my chair. up the hill. for the doctor. beautifully. etc.
subject (3rd person singular, etc)	**be-verb**	**main verb**	**completion**
She/He It The man That girl The water etc.	is	doing raining. trying to doing boiling. etc.	the cleaning. open the door. her homework. etc.

A present continuous sentence without a time phrase usually implies that the action is taking place at the time the sentence is uttered; so 'I am writing' implies 'now'. However, there are time indicators that might be added at the beginning or end of the sentence, more as an emphasis: **now, right now, at the moment**, *etc. Look at these sentences.*

statement	time indicator
I'm sitting at my desk	now. /right now. /at the moment.
time indicator	**statement**
At the moment, /Now, /Right now,	I'm sitting at my desk.

STATIVE VERBS:

*This is a good place to introduce Stative verbs. Stative verbs don't normally take the suffix ~***ing***. They are used in their present or past simple forms. These verbs don't imply an action, as the name suggests. However, don't be fooled, like everything else in the English language exceptions are lurking about. Here are some common Stative verbs and their* **incorrect** *usage.*

Stative verb	incorrect sentence
know understand like have seem etc.	I am **knowing** him. I am **understanding** this lesson. I am **liking** this lesson. I am **having** a car. He is **seeming** very tired. etc.

And here are some examples of dual usage of Stative verbs.

Stative	continuous
I **feel** tired. He **looks** happy. She **smells** delightful. I **have** two children. He **is** a teacher.	I **am feeling** tired. He **is looking** happy. She **is smelling** the rose. I **am having** dinner at the moment. She **is having** twins. *(giving birth to)* He **is being** a nuisance.

PRESENT CONTINUOUS passive

The present continuous passive is made by combining the **present continuous be-verb** *and the* **3ʳᵈ/past participle** *(regular and irregular verbs). The present continuous be-verb indicates that the process (action) is occurring at the moment; it has the characteristic of the present continuous. Time indicators such as;* **now**, **right now**, **at the moment**, **today**, *etc., may be used. With future time the event occurs in the future. The sentences look like this:*

object	verb	3ʳᵈ/past participle	by subject (completion)
1ˢᵗ person = I	**am being**	taken taught chased made	to school by bus. to be polite. in New Zealand. for a walk.
3ʳᵈ person = He, She, It **singular = The dog, My** car, Peter, etc. **uncountables =** Cheese, Petroleum, etc.	**is being**	sold bought walked grown played shown read drunk	some interesting paintings. all over the world. in Muslim countries. how to use the toilet. to the zoo. by the cat. from left to right. to the park after school.
2ⁿᵈ person = You **plurals = The apples,** These cars, Her children, They, etc.	**are being**	produced stolen given asked etc.	in the Middle-East. by the dog. in the market place. etc.

Now let's combine these four segments into sentences.

I**'m being taken** to school by bus.
Petroleum **is being produced** in the Middle-East.
Carpets **are being made** in the market place.
This coffee **is being drunk** all over the world.
I **am being shown** some interesting paintings.
The children **are being taken** to the zoo.
The cat **is being chased** by the dog.
This book **is being read** all over the world.
The children **are being shown** how to use the toilet.

PAST CONTINUOUS active

The past continuous is formed by using a **be-verb**, *a* **main verb** *plus* ~**ing**. *The past continuous expresses an elongated time period just as the present continuous does, but in the past. The past continuous is seldom on its own but has an accompanying action which usually occurs within it. One way to describe it is to say that it is a big picture which contains a smaller one. There can also be two actions occurring side by side or simultaneously.*

In the past continuous we use two be-verbs; **was** (*with* **I, he, she, it, singular** *and* **uncountables nouns**). *And* **were** (*with* **you, they, we,** *and* **plurals**).

The main verb undergoes the same changes as in the present continuous. This is where the similarity with the present continuous ends.

Here are the three possible combinations of two events of any nature that can be described by the use of the past continuous, using these three conjunctions; **when, while, as.**

1. **Past continuous** *plus* **past simple**.
2. **Past continuous** *plus* **past continuous**.
3. **Past simple** *plus* **past continuous**.

To carry the analogy of the two pictures further; we might say that these three conjunctions are the nails that hold the pictures up. **As** *and* **while** *hold up the bigger picture;* **when** *holds up the smaller, inner, picture. These words can also start the sentence, in which case a comma is put between the two sentences. Look at these sentences.*

1. **While** they **were sitting** on their porch**,** a car **drove** across their lawn. They **were sitting** on their porch **when** a car **drove** across their lawn.

2. **As** they **were rowing** up the river**,** their manager **was following** them in his car. Their manager **was following** them in his car **as** they **were rowing** up the river.

3. They **heard** the explosion **while** they **were having** dinner.

    When they **heard** the explosion, they **were having** dinner.

The past continuous can also be used with specific time that suggest a long duration, i.e., **2007, 20th century, 1990s,** *etc.*

What **were** you **doing** in **2001**?
The world **was fighting** major wars in the **20th century**.
She **was living** in Latvia in the **1970s**.

PAST CONTINUOUS passive
The past continuous passive is made by combining the **past continuous be-verb** *and the* **3rd/past participle** *(regular and irregular verbs). The past continuous be-verb indicates that the process (action) is occurring in conjunction with some other action just as in the past continuous active. It contains all the characteristics of the past continuous sentence, except the verb formation. The sentences look like this:*

object	verb	3rd/past participle	by subject (completion)
1st person = I **3rd person** = He, She, It **singular** = The dog, My car, Peter, etc. **uncountables** = Cheese, Petroleum, etc. **2nd person** = You **plurals** = The apples, These cars, Her children, They, etc.	was being were being	taken taught chased made sold bought kept played shown read drunk produced stolen etc.	to school by bus. in New Zealand. when I first saw her. some interesting paintings. all over the world. we lay by the pool. when he hit the wall. in cool cellars. to the zoo when the rain began. when the lights went out. in the Middle-East. in the market place. etc.

Now let's combine some of these four segments into sentences.

The boys **were being taken** to the zoo when the rain began.
While the lunch **was being made**, we lay by the pool.
The pickpocket **was being chased** when he hit the wall.
Cheese **was being sold** in the market place.
The wine **was being kept** in cool cellars.
The children **were being put** to bed when the lights went out.
She **was being shown** the school when I first saw her.

PRESENT PERFECT active

The present simple indicators are the auxiliary verbs, **have** *and* **has**. *The past simple indicators are the ~ed and the* **irregular** *verbs in their* **3rd/past participle** *forms. So the present perfect sentence is formed by combining the auxiliary verb* **have** *or* **has** *with the* **3rd/past participle** *(regular and irregular verbs).*

The present perfect is an interesting concept. It is, to put it one way, a combination of the 'present simple' concept and the 'past simple' concept. It expresses an action that definitely occurred in the past but its residue has continued to the present.

One way we get this continuity is through our memory: any action we remember can be expressed in this way, as long as **we don't feel the need to state a specific time**. *We use this sentence structure to express our experiences.*

Action taken in time that is yet unfinished can also be expressed through the present perfect. There are two types of time expressions we can use; we can indicate the starting point of the action and we can state the duration of the action but we cannot specify a moment in time; i.e.
I have seen this film ~~yesterday~~. *The time indicator 'yesterday' is too specific for the present perfect.*

Had all things been equal; the English language would have standardized all its verbs, but that is not to be, hence we have:

base verbs	3rd person verbs	past simple verbs	3rd/past participle verbs
be	is	was	been
play	plays	played	played
walk	walks	walked	walked
cut	cuts	cut	cut
become	becomes	became	become
go	goes	went	gone

Not to mention the present continuous verbs, or verbs with plural subjects! With the present perfect we are only concerned with the verbs in the 4th column, even though with the ~ed ending verbs it seems as though we are using the past simple verbs. So, present perfect sentences look like this:

The teacher **has entered** the class.
The students **have done** their homework.
I **haven't seen** Peter today.

The present perfect time indicators (adverbs of time) are:

Unfinished time

statement	time indicator	duration
I have talked to my teacher	**today.**	
I have read two books	**this***	week.
Toyota has sold the most cars		year.
She has walked 200 kilometres		morning.
etc.		etc.

*'this' *put before a duration of time word suggests that the time is unfinished.*

The starting point of an action (the action has not come to an end).

statement	preposition (time indicator)	time/phrase
I have lived in New Zealand	**since**	1980.
I have lived in the same house		I was a boy.
She has worked as a journalist		she left school.
I haven't played football		I broke my leg.
etc.		etc.

The duration of an action (up to the point at which the statement is made).

statement	preposition (time indicator)	duration
I have lived in New Zealand I have lived in the same house She has worked as a journalist I haven't eaten an ice cream etc.	for	30 years. 45 years. 25 years. 2 weeks. etc.

Actions that are repeated.

statement	repetitions
I have read *Great Expectations* I have had Liverpool has scored etc.	**several** times. **four** cups of coffee this morning. **two** goals so far*. *(The game hasn't ended)*. etc.

*'so far' *indicates up to the point the statement is made.*

There are six specific adverbs used with the present perfect. **See pages 32 and 75.**

PRESENT PERFECT passive

The present perfect passive is made by combining **have/has** *and the* **3rd/ past participle be-verb** *and the* **3rd/past participle** *(regular and irregular verbs). The present perfect passive contains all the characteristics of the active form. Look at these sentences.*

object	verb	3rdpast participle	by subject (completion)
1st person = I **2nd person** = You **plurals** = The apples, These cars, Her children, They, etc. **3rd person** = He, She, It **singular** = The dog, My car, Peter, etc. **uncountables** = Cheese, Petroleum, etc.	**have been** **has been**	taken taught sold bought grown played shown read drunk asked etc.	to school by bus. to be polite. in Japan. some interesting paintings. all over the world. to the zoo. to the park after school. a lot of questions. in the market place. etc.

Now let's combine some of these four segments into sentences.

The children **have been taught** to be polite.
Peter **has been asked** a lot of questions.
The painting **has been sold** in the market place.
The children **have been taken** to the park after school.
Football **has been played** all over the world for a very long time. Charles Dickens **has been read** all over the world.

PAST PERFECT active
The past perfect is an interesting chronological concept. It is meant to indicate the occurrence of an event before another event which has also occurred in the past. However, this can be done more simply, in most instances, by the past simple using the conjunctions/adverbs **before** *and* **after.**

The past perfect is formed by combining the past auxiliary verb **had** *with the 3rd/past participle (regular or irregular) verb. Because the sentence has a reference point in time it is usually accompanied by another sentence in the same way that the past continuous sentence is.*

In explaining this grammatical concept, I equate the past simple as a wall and everything occurring **'behind'** *it as the past perfect. Look at this information.*

I **came** to New Zealand in **1980 (The wall).** Before that time I **had done** many things.

I presented an English language TV programme.
I taught English at the Iranian Air Force.
I did my military service.

Now I can combine the **'wall'** *sentence to what I had done before that time.*

I **had presented** an English language programme *before* I **came** to New Zealand.
I **had taught** at the Iranian Air Force *before* I **came** to New Zealand.
I **had done** my military service *before* I **came** to New Zealand.
I taught at the Iranian Air force *after* I **had done** my military service.

I can also put these sentences in their chronological order.

I **had done** my military service *before* I **taught** at the Iranian Air Force.
I **had taught** at the Iranian Air force *before* I **presented** an English Language TV programme.

Since **after** *and* **before** *are time indicators, we can avoid using the past perfect and make the simpler sentence using two past simple sentences. Look at these sentences.*

I **presented** an English language TV programme *before* I **came** to New Zealand.
I **taught** at the Iranian Air force *before* I **presented** an English language TV programme.
I **did** my military service *before* I **taught** at the Iranian Air force.

Here are other conjunctions that can be used with past perfect sentences; **when**, **by the time**, **because**, **until**, **since**. *With the exception of* **since**, *the other conjunctions can be put at the beginning of the sentence or between the two sentences. Look at these sentences.*

conjunction	sentence
When	the sun had come out, we went to the park.
By the time	the rain had stopped, we were soaking wet.
Because	we had arrived late, we missed the opening speech.
Until	I was 27, I hadn't smoked.

sentence	conjunction	sentence
We went to the park	**when**	the sun had come out.
We were soaking wet	**by the time**	the sun had come out.
We had missed the opening speech	**because**	we had arrived late.
I hadn't smoked	**until**	I was 27.
I hadn't been back	**since**	I left.

Here are some more sentences.

I realized I **had seen** this film **when** I **was** on the plane to Los Angeles.
The train **had left by the time** I **got** to the station.
By the time I **got** to the station, the train **had left**.
The florist **had left** the flowers at the back door **because** he **knew** no one was home.

Because the florist **knew** no one was home, he **had left** the flowers at the back door.
We **hadn't recognized** him **until** he **took off** his moustache.
Until he **took off** his moustache, we **hadn't recognized** him.
I **hadn't seen** him **since** we **were** children.

Keep in mind that some of these sentences might also be used in the past simple.

PAST PERFECT passive
The past perfect passive is made by combining **had** *and the* **3rd/past participle be-verb** *and the* **3rd/past participle** *(regular and irregular verbs). The present perfect passive contains all the characteristics of the active form. Look at these sentences.*

object	verb	3rd/past participle	by subject (completion)
1st person = I **2nd person** = You **plurals** = The apples, These cars, Her children, They, etc. **3rd person** = He, She, It **singular** = The dog, My car, Peter, etc. **uncountables** = Cheese, Petroleum, etc.	**had been**	taken taught sold bought walked grown played shown read drunk asked etc.	to school by bus. to be polite. in Japan. some interesting paintings. under poor conditions. to the zoo when I was a child. for the school. by the cat. to the park after school. at the meeting. in the market place. etc.

Now let's combine these four segments into sentences.

The children **had been taught** to be polite.
You **had been shown** some very interesting paintings.
The game **had been played** under poor conditions.
A lot of questions **had been asked** at the meeting.
Last year, a lot of cars **had been produced** in Japan.

PRESENT PERFECT CONTINUOUS active
I refer to the present perfect continuous as our **shadow.** *Just as we are unable to separate ourselves from our shadow; the present perfect continuous keeps us well-connected to the action we are talking about. We cannot dislocate ourselves from the action which started in the past; unlike the present perfect which in one of its functions can be a part of the past.*

The grammatical formation of this sentence is the combination of the present perfect and the present continuous. **Because the be-verb is required in both the present perfect and the present continuous forms** *we use the* **3rd/past participle** *form of the* **be-verb** *as in the present perfect:* **have/has been** *and the continuous verb;* **main-verb** *plus* **~ing** *and we get:* **have been living; has been living**. *We could say that the base* **be-verb** *is embedded in the* **3rd/past participle be-verb been**.

These sentences are usually completed with the use of the prepositions **since** *and* **for**. *Look at these sentences*

subject (1st & 2nd persons, plurals, etc)		continuous	completion
I You They The boys The Smiths etc.	**have been**	living waiting coming holidaying travelling etc.	here *since* 2000. here *for* 13 years. for the bus *since* 2 o'clock. here *since* 2005. here *for* a long time. etc.
subject (3rd person, singular, uncountables)		continuous	completion
He She Peter The girl The rain etc.	**has been**	living waiting dancing falling travelling etc.	here *since* 2000. here *for* 13 years. for the bus *since* 2 o'clock. *since* she was 12. for two hours. etc.

The HERE and NOW

There are times when the present perfect and the present perfect continuous convey the same time period. I call this the **HERE** *and* **NOW**.

I am living in New Zealand at the moment *(now)*.
I live in New Zealand *(here)*.
So I can use both the present perfect and the present perfect continuous to express this information.

I have lived in New Zealand for 30 years.
I have been living in New Zealand for 30 years.

In the next two sentences, the first one has no time duration so it's in the past; the second has a different place, it's not here (New Zealand), so it too is in the past.

I have lived in Iran. (*This has been one of my experiences.*)
*I have lived in Iran for 25 years. (*I'm not in Iran now, so it also is a past experience.*)

*He doesn't box any more, but he has boxed for 17 years. (*boxing is a past experience.*)
She is still teaching; She's been teaching since she was 20. (*teaching is a continuous experience to this day.*)

They moved to Australia 2 years ago, they are still there.
They have lived in Ausralia for 2 years.
They have been living in Australia for two years.

We know they are still in Australia so both the second and third sentences convey the same idea, a sense of **now**.

*Some would say these sentences would be better expressed in the past simple.

PRESENT PERFECT CONTINUOUS passive

This is an awkward grammatical construct and is not used frequently. As the examples will testify, one wouldn't be making frequent use of it.

I **have been being** shown this painting for the tenth time.
This book **has been being** printed for the last ten years.

PAST PERFECT CONTINUOUS active

The past perfect continuous, in some ways, is similar to the past simple continuous and can be substituted, in some instances, by the past simple continuous. Another way to look at it is to see it as a present perfect continuous sentence in the past. Look at these two sentences:

Peter **had been living** in Paris when the war began.
Peter **was living** in Paris when the war began.

Here the two sentences have almost the same meaning and time frame. To differentiate these two tenses something else is required. Look at these sentences:

I could tell John **had been smoking**; there were cigarette butts in the ashtray.
I could tell John **was smoking**; there were cigarette butts in the ashtray.

To say that **John was smoking** *means that I saw him smoking so I do not need to surmise (could tell) nor do I need the evidence (cigarette butts in the ashtray).*

In the first sentence John **wasn't** *smoking when I saw him. He* **had been smoking <u>before</u>** *I saw him.*

So the past perfect continuous suggests that the action was either over or was about to be over when the other action occurred; there is a sequence here where the past perfect continuous action occurs before the past simple action. Compare these sentences:

Peter **had been working** very long hours so he decided to change his job.
Peter **had been planning** his holidays when he fell ill.

To these sentences:

Peter **was working** very long hours so he decided to change his job.
Peter **was planning** his holidays when he fell ill.

The second two sentences suggest that the two actions contained in each sentence occurred simultaneously or almost simultaneously.

The grammatical structure is steady and is not influenced by the subject.

all subjects	pst per	continuous	(completion)
I You	had been	living cooking	in Spain during the war. when the fire started.

FUTURE active

The first thing to make clear here is that the English language **does not have** *a future tense. There are future intentions galore, but* **no** *future tense. The present tenses, simple and continuous, serve their own functions as explained; but as also explained when a future time is added to these sentences, a concrete future is indicated. Without the future time the sentence expresses an intent, a sense of perpetuity or the present. Look at these sentences.*

I will (am going to) buy a car. *(intent)*
I go to school. *(prolonged present action)*
I'm going to the park. *(at this moment)*

Almost all the modals and semi-modals can be used with future time to indicate future actions. Look at these sentences:

without future time	with future time.
I play tennis.* I am playing tennis.** I will play tennis. I can play tennis.*** I would play tennis. I ought to play tennis.**** I have to play tennis. I'm going to play tennis. I'll have finished this book ***** etc.	tomorrow afternoon. etc. **+Any other future time will project these actions into the future, making them most likely to happen.** by Saturday.

*this is something I do.
**this is something I'm doing at the moment.
***this is something I know how to do.
****this is something I advise myself to do.
*****this is something I anticipate finishing in the stated future.
+I play tennis tomorrow afternoon.
+I'm playing tennis tomorrow afternoon.

will and going to

The difference between **will** *and* **going to***: as I see it,* **will** *expresses an unconsidered decision whereas* **going to** *suggests a decision arrived at after some consideration. Look at this, albeit, contrived conversation:*

Albert: What are you doing tonight?
Jerry: Nothing that I know of. No plans.
Albert: Would you like to go to a movie with me?
Jerry: Now that's a good idea. **I'll** go to a movie with you.
(Enter another friend)
Chris: Jerry, are you doing anything tonight?
Jerry: Yes, I'm **going to** see a movie with Albert.

FUTURE passive

As we have seen passive sentences always contain the **be-verb** *in some form; this is also true of future passive sentences. It is also possible to make passive sentences in all the tense forms. However, only three forms are more commonly used to make the future passive;* **will***,* **going to** *and the* **present perfect***. Look at these sentences.*

This building **will be** finished in ten years time. *(anticipated conclusion)*
This building **is going to be** finished in ten years time. *(intention)*
This building **will have been** finished in ten years time. *(certain conclusion)*

Other sentences are also possible; however, they can be a bit cumbersome. Look at these sentences.

This building **will be going to be** finished next year.
This building **will be being** finished by this time next year.
By this time next year, this building **will have been being** finished for one year.

Quite unusable, don't you think?

PART 4
Other Grammatical Structures

CONDITIONAL SENTENCES

*Generally, conditional sentences are divided into four categories: statements of fact (**Zero conditionals**); possibilities under certain conditions (**First conditionals**); expressions of wish or hope (**Second conditionals**); and situations which might have been, which also express regret (**Third conditionals**).*

*Conditional sentences always consist of two sentences joined by a conjunction; which is often put at the beginning of the sentence and the two sentences are separated by a comma. The conjunction can also take the conventional position of being in between the two sentences. The sentence containing the condition is headed by **if**.*

One of these sentences contains a condition or situation, the other contains an outcome of the condition or situation, which can be real, unlikely, hoped for or contrary to the actual statement.

*The most common conjunctions used in these sentences are **if** and **unless**. **When** might be used when describing regular activities.*

There are other ways of expressing conditional sentences; here we will deal only with the more common ways with a passing reference to the others.

***Zero conditionals** state a fact or a regular occurrence. When there is no other possible outcome from a particular action we use the **Zero conditional** to express it. Similarly, when a repetitive outcome can be assured, the **Zero conditional** is used.*

This is the grammatical structure of the Zero conditional.

	subj	prs verb	completion,	subj	prs verb	completion.
If	you	add	2 and 2,	you	get	4.
	you	drop	oil on water,	the oil	floats.	
	there	is	a documentary on TV,	I	watch	it.
	Peter	goes	for a run,	he	feels	better.
	they	are invited	to dinner,	they	always bring	a dessert.

There are some things that happen or that people do on a regular basis. These occurrences or activities are often accompanied by other regular events or activities; in these instances the use of **when** *is more likely than* **if**. *Look at these sentences;*

When* the sun rises, the earth begins to warm up.
When she gets home from work, she phones her mother.
Whenever* I phone my ex-wife, she invites me to dinner.
Whenever I go to a friend's for dinner, I always take a bottle of wine.

***When** is a regular occurrence;* **whenever** *is an occasional occurrence and therefore serves almost in the same way as* **if**.
While the **Zero conditional**, *generally, uses no modals, the other three conditionals do.*

The **First conditionals** *use* **will**, **can**, **may** *and* **might***; the* **Second conditionals** *use* **would**, **could** *and* **might***; the* **Third conditionals** *also use* **would**, **could** *and* **might**.

First conditional *sentences are, in a way, dependent sentences; in that the action intended depends on the circumstance that occurs first. Does this make sense? The part that is meant to happen first is called the conditional and is introduced by the conjunction* **if**.

Will *suggests a high probability;*
Can *suggests an ability or a possibility;*
May *suggests a 50/50 likelihood;*
Might *suggests a less likelihood than* **may**.

This is the grammatical structure of the First conditional.

	subj	prs verb	completion,	subj	modal	base verb	completion
If	I	am invited	to her party,	I	'll	go	alone.
	they	arrive	in time,	we	can	sit down	to dinner on time.
	he	sees	her before 6 pm,	he	may	take	her to the cinema.
	the boys	miss	the bus,	you	might	pick them up	from the bus stop.
	you	hurry,		you	won't	miss	the bus.
	Peter	asks	Mary,	she	won't	refuse.	

Here are some **First conditionals**:

If I'm invited to her party, If they arrive on time,
If he sees her before 6 pm, If she misses the bus,

We are not sure of these events; they may happen or they may not. However, should they happen, there are a variety of actions that may be taken in each instance. Let's look at some possibilities.

If I'm invited to her party,

> I'll go alone.
> I can take a bottle of wine.
> I may wear my red dress.

If they arrive on time,

> we'll be able to sit down to dinner on time.
> they can see the beginning of the race.
> I might take them for a drive.

If he sees her before 6 pm,

> he may invite her to his house.
> he won't have the present ready.

If she misses the bus,

> he won't be waiting for her.
> she might have to take a taxi.
> she can return home.

*The modal **should** can replace **if** in **First conditional** sentences. Look at these sentences.*

Should I be invited to her party, I'll go alone.
Should they arrive on time, we'll be able to sit down to dinner on time.
Should she miss the bus, she can return home.

These sentences can also be used to construct requests. They have a formal quality often used in business letter. Look at these sentences.

Should you see Peter, could you ask him to call me?
Should you be unable to attend, please let us know.
Should Mary need a lift, call us.
Should you decide to go out, take the keys with you.

The above sentences could also be used in this way. Look at these sentences.

If I **should** be invited to her party, I'll go alone.
If they **should** arrive on time, we'll be able to sit down to dinner on time.

And here are some sentences with the other modals in the conditional sentence.

If you **could** come home early, we might go to a movie.
The children **would** be very happy **if** you **would** tell them a story.
If you **will** continue to talk in class, I**'ll** have to ask you to leave.

Second conditionals *are used to state a desire which is not likely to be fulfilled at the moment; but certain conditions might make it possible in the future. The likelihood is that the condition needed will not be achieved. These sentences have no reality, only wishes and desires, even though they are expressed in the past tense form, they indicate the future.*

This is the grammatical structure of the Second conditional.

	subj	pts verb	completion,	subj	modal	base verb	completion
If	you	practised	more,	you	would	get	better.
	they	hurried,		they	wouldn't	miss	the train,
	he	wanted to marry	her,	he	needed to	be	more hardworking.
	it	rained	later,	the picnic	could	be	ruined.
	Peter	asked	Mary,	she	might	say,	'Yes'.

Would *and* **could** *carry the same implications as* **will** *and* **can***; however,* **might** *implies less likelihood than* **may**.

Here are some **Second conditionals***:*

If Peter had the money,
If the price of houses dropped,
If I wanted to buy a car,
If Mary married him,

These sentences state conditions that do not exist at the moment; had they existed certain possibilities would have opened up; however, at the moment they are highly unlikely. Look at these sentences;

If Peter had the money,

> he would buy the house.
> he could take a holiday.

If the price of houses dropped,

> more people could own their own homes.
> there would be more money to buy food.

If I wanted to buy a car,

> I would buy a Toyota.
> I would put money aside.

If Mary married him,

> she might live in Canada.
> he would give her a diamond ring.
> her parents wouldn't be happy.

A **Second conditional** *anomaly is the use of* **were** *instead of* **was**. *This is a formal use of the* **Second conditional** *and is preferred in some quarters. So:*

If I **were** you*, I'd be careful of what I say.
If he **were** to come, I'd pass on your message.

'If I were you/he/she/they/Peter/Mary' is generally used to make a suggestion or give advice, as in the first sentence.
The object pronoun can be both in the subject form (I**/**he**/**she**/etc) or the object (**me**/**him**/**her**/etc) form. **Were** can also be used in conjunction with these phrases. The first verb in the sentence may be in any tense.*

He speaks *as if* he **were** a doctor.
She walked in *as though* she **were** the Queen of Sheba.

Third conditionals *are not what they seem; however, they are truly in the past. The events stated in the sentences either happened or didn't happen; generally, affirmative concepts imply negative outcomes and vice versa.*

This is the grammatical structure of the Third conditional.

	subj	ptp verb	completion,	subj	modal	pp verb	completion
If	you	had practised	more,	you	would	have got	better.
	Peter	had hurried,		he	wouldn't	have missed	the train,
	he	had genuinely wanted to marry	her,	he	would	have been	more persuasive.
	it	had rained	later,	the picnic	could	have been	ruined.
	Peter	had asked	Mary,	she	might	have said	'Yes'.

So what do these sentences mean?

The first sentence means – you didn't practise so you didn't get better.
The second sentence means – Peter didn't hurry so he missed the train.
And so on...
Now we can say the same thing using the word **had**. *Look at these sentences.*

Had you practised more, you'd have got better.
Had they hurried, they wouldn't have missed the train.
Had he wanted to marry her, he would have been more persuasive.

CONDITIONAL Questions
The non-conditional part of the sentence is used to form questions. Look at these sentences.

If you find a lot of money on the street, **what will you do with it?**
If you found a lot of money on the street, **would you give it to the police?**
What would you have done with the money if you had found a lot of it (money) on the street?
Would you give the money to the police if you found a lot of it (money) on the street?

UNLESS

Unless is the other side of the coin. It's basically like scratching your left ear with your right hand from behind your head. It serves the same purpose as **if** *but it's a bit awkward. However, it does carry an undertone of a warning or threat.*

This is the grammatical structure with unless.

	subj	prs verb	completion,	subj	modal	base verb	completion
Unless	he	pays	his fine,	he	'll	lose	his car.
	it	rains,		we	'll	go	to the zoo.
	you	shut up,		you	'll have to	leave	the room.
	you	eat	your dinner,	you	won't	get	any dessert.
	she	gives	me my money,	I	'll	tell	the police.
	Mary	trains	harder,	she	won't	win	the match.
	I	say	I'm sorry,	she	will	ignore	me.

Just to compare **if** *with* **unless.**

Unless he pays his fine, he'll lose his car. =

> **If** he *doesn't* pay his fine, he'll lose his car.
>
> **If** he pays his fine, he *won't* lose his car.

Unless it rains, we'll go to the zoo. =

> **If** it *doesn't* rain, we'll go to the zoo.
>
> **If** it rains, we *won't* go to the zoo.

Unless you shut up, you'll have to leave the room. =

> **If** you *don't* shut up, you'll have to leave the room.
>
> **If** you shut up, you *won't* have to leave the room.

Mixed CONDITIONALS

Mixed conditionals *are used to express two different time frames within one sentence. Easier said than done! There are six possible combinations of mixed conditionals:*

past + present
past + future
present + past
present + future
future + past

future + present

Here are some examples of these mixed conditionals, as you will notice not all of them quite 'gel'.

past + present
If he **hadn't drunk** so much, he**'d know** where his car is.
If he **had been** rude to the police, he**'d be** in custody now.

past + future
If she **married** him, she**'ll** have to live on a farm..
If they **came** to the party, I**'ll** be very happy.

present + past
If I **were** interested in maths, **I'd have been** a maths teacher.
If she **were** truly happy, she **wouldn't have been** on drugs.

present + future
If you **train** more, you**'d be** a better player.
If you **read*** more, your vocabulary **would** increase.
In the present simple

future + past
If I **were going to** the wedding, **I'd have hired** a tuxedo.
If I **weren't intending to buy** a house, **I'd have gone** on holiday.

future + present
If she **were coming** out with me tonight, **I'd be** very happy.
If Peter **doesn't come** to the party, Mary **would be** very annoyed.

Good luck, anyway!

GERUNDS

*Gerunds are ~**ing** words that are not accompanied by **be-verbs**. They are used as **adjectives** and **abstract nouns**. Some gerunds in the noun form can take the plural form, e.g., **leavings**, **writings**, etc.*

They can be used in the subject or object position and can be the object of preposition. Look at these sentences.

Swimming is very good exercise. *(abstract noun)*
I go to the **swimming** pool twice a week. *(adjective)*
She likes **shopping** in a **shopping** mall. *(abstract noun and adjective)*
They were excited about **going** on holiday. *(after preposition)*

They can also come after a noun when used in truncated relative clauses. Look at these sentences.

The man who is **standing** by the window is a doctor.
The man **standing** by the window is a doctor. *(truncated relative clause)*
Here are some verbs that are usually followed by gerunds.

admit	avoid	(can't bear)	(can't stand)	consider	deny
recommend	enjoy	finish	keep	mind	miss	practise
quit	suggest	dislike			

Look at these sentences.

He admitted **stealing** the car.
I can't bear **eating** snails.
She finished **reading** that book at 2.00 am.
The Smiths are considering **buying** that house.
John didn't deny **hitting** Peter.
Would you mind **passing** the sugar?
I quit **smoking** 25 years ago.

INDIRECT OR REPORTED SPEECH

In English we sometimes distinguish between what someone actually says; that is, we repeat the exact words they have spoken or we adjust them slightly. This adjustment is referred to as **indirect** *or* **reported speech**.

Probably the most frequent use of the indirect speech is when we repeat what we ourselves have said or thought.

These reported speech sentences consist of two parts; the first part contains the **reporting verb** *and the second part contains the* **reported clause**. *The tense of the reported clause is dependent on the tense of the reporting clause. The sentence below is an example of a reported sentence.*

<u>He said (that)</u> *he enjoyed playing football.*

The underlined words contain the reporting verb, reporting clause, while the italicized part is the reported clause. The original sentence looks like this:

He said, 'I enjoy playing football.'

The repetition of the exact words of a speaker is most frequent in a court of law or other situations where accuracy is necessary. Otherwise, the reported version is in more common use.

Here are some of the more common reporting verbs and their use.

say	make a statement
tell*	give information or an order
ask*	ask a question, make a polite request
advise*	make a serious suggestion
inform*	give information
order*	to give a command
state	make a statement
complain	express a dissatisfaction with something
suggest	offer an idea
request	ask for something
demand	assert a need
wonder	be curious about something
reply	answer a question, respond to a situation
insist	demand

*These words are usually followed by a proper noun or pronoun.

There are four types of reported clauses; 'that'-clauses (statements); 'to' infinites (commands); 'if'/'whether' (closed) and 'Wh-' (open) questions.

There are some rules to be followed to give this process uniformity; however, as with almost all the rules of English grammar, some exceptions are likely to be found.

The tense of the reporting verb controls the subsequent verbs. The present simple and the present continuous cause no change in the subsequent verbs. All past tenses cause one step back into the past; however, nothing goes further back than the past perfect.
Quotation marks and question marks are not used in the reported form nor is the comma after the reporting clause.

Verbs after **'to'** *are usually base verbs and therefore experience no change.* **'to'** *can follow* **wh-**
questions and always follows reported imperative speech. Look at these sentences.

He told me where **to** go.
He told me what **to** buy.
He ordered us **to** leave the room.
He ordered us **to** sit down.

Reported **closed** *questions are prefaced by* **'if'** *or* **'whether'**; *Reported* **open** *questions are prefaced by the relevant* **wh-word**. **Whether** *is more likely to be used if there is a suggestion of a choice.*

The reported clause in the question form changes into the statement form. The auxiliary verbs **do**, **does** *and* **did** *are not used in the reported clause; the other auxiliary and modal verbs are.*

It is not always necessary to change **must** *to* **had to**.

The **'I'** *in the direct speech always refers to the speaker.* **'You'** *would, generally, refer to the person spoken to. A third person reporting will also change the pronouns in the reported sentence. Now let's look as some examples.*

Persons in **direct** speech.	Persons in **indirect** speech.
Mary said, '**You** are a fool.'	Mary said (told **me**) **I** was a fool.
Mary said, '**I** am a fool.'	Mary said (told me) **she** was a fool.
Mary said, '**Peter** is a fool.'	Mary said (told me) **Peter** was a fool.
Mary said, '**Peter** is a fool.'	Mary said (told me) **you** were a fool. (*Speaking to Peter*)
Mary said, '**Peter** is a fool.'	Peter (said) told Mary you (had) said **I** was a fool. (*Peter speaking to Mary*)
Mary said, '**John** is a fool.'	Peter (said) told me Mary (had) said **John** was a fool. (a *third person speaking*)

*Let's look at the **tense** changes.*
*These **direct speech** statements change to these **reported speech** statements.*

She says, 'I **drink** wine.'	She says she **drinks** wine.
She is saying, 'I **drink** wine.'	She is saying she **drinks** wine.

Note: *There is no change in the tense form.*

*Now look at these sentences where the **reporting verb** is in the **past tense**.*

She **said**, 'I **drink** wine.'	She said she **drank** wine.
She **said**, 'I **drank** wine.'	She said she **had drunk** wine.
She **said**, 'I **have drunk** wine.'	She said she **had drunk** wine.
She **said**, 'I **had drunk** wine.'	She said she **had drunk** wine.

Note: *All three past sentences are the same in the reported form. So how do we distinguish the **past simple** from the **present perfect** and the **past perfect**?*

*Generally, the **past simple** will have a **past time** connected to it, either in the question or statement preceding it or in the statement itself. The **present perfect** will **not** have a **past time**. So the **past simple** sentence should be something like this:*

She **said**, 'I **drank** beer *at the party.*'
And the reported statement would look like this:
She **said** she **had drunk** beer *at the party*.*
**'at the party' is a past event.*

So how do we distinguish between the **past simple** *and the* **past perfect***? Fortunately, we don't need to, because, generally, in most everyday usage, the* **past perfect** *can be substituted by the* **past simple***.*

She **said**, 'I **drank** beer at the party.'   She **said**, 'I **had drunk** beer at the party.'

If we use the second statement, I doubt whether we will be asked for a grammatical clarification. And some people might simply say; 'She **said** *she* **drank** *beer at the party.' and let grammatical correctness fall by the wayside.*

Now let's look at the two **question** *forms. When questions are transformed into the reported form,* ***they change into the statement form***. *Look at these question grids.*

Closed questions.
1.   Direct question.

reporting verb clause*	question		
She asked me,	'Are	you	a teacher?'

Reported question.

*rvc	conjunction	subject	verb	object
she asked me	if	I	was	a teacher.

2.   Direct question.

*rvc	question			
She asked me,	'Have	you	seen	*Life of Pi?'*

Reported question.

*rvc	conjunction	subject	verb	object
She asked me	if	I	had seen	*Life of Pi.*

3.   Direct question.

*rvc	question			
She asked me,	'Do	you	play	tennis?'

Reported question.

*rvc	conjunction	subject	verb	object
She asked me	if	I	played	tennis.

4. Direct question.

*rvc	question			
She asked me,	'Can	you	play	tennis?'

Reported question.

*rvc	conjunction	subject	verb	object
She asked me	**if**	I	could play	tennis.

Note: *There has been a change in pronouns and in the third example there is no 'do' in the reported segment. In the fourth example note the change from* **can** *to* **could**.

Now take a look at **open questions.**

Open question.

1. Direct question.

*rvc	question			
She asked me,	'Where	did	you	live	in Iran?'

Reported question

*rvc	question word	subject	verb	object
She asked me	**where**	I	had lived	in Iran.

2. Direct question.

*rvc	question			
She asked me,	'Which book	have	you	just	read?'

Reported question.

*rvc	question word + noun	subject	verb	adv	verb
She asked me	which book	I	had	just	read.

3. Direct question

*rvc	question		
She asked me,	'How old	is	your father?'

Reported question.

*rvc	question word + adj	subject	verb
She asked me	how old	my father	was.

This pattern is followed with all the open questions. Here are some further examples.

She asked me **where** she could buy a pair of shoes.
The students asked the teacher **when** the next exam was.
The officer asked us **what** we had in our bags.

Now look at **imperative** *reported sentences.*

The teacher said, 'Sit down!'	The teacher **told** us **to** sit down.
The doctor said, 'Please sit down.'	The doctor **asked** me **to** sit down.
He said, 'Could you pass the sugar?'	He **asked** me **to** pass the sugar.
The officer said, 'Leave the room!'	The officer **commanded** them **to** leave the room.

Now look at these **imperatives**.

'Go to that shop.'	She told me **where to** go.
'Ask that man.'	She told me **who to** ask.
'Take the book.'	She told me **what to** take.
'Take this book.'	She told me **which** book to take.
'You should buy this house.'	She advised me **which** house **to** buy.

In **negative** *imperatives* **not** *is put before* **to**.

'Don't touch that glass!'	He ordered us **not** to touch that glass.
'Don't be late.'	He told us **not** to be late.
'Peter, please don't shout.'	She asked Peter **not** to shout.

Now we come to the tricky part; designating time to reported speech. If the conversation or statement is being repeated on the day it was spoken, there will be no time change. For instance;

Today.	**Today.**
Mary said, 'I arrived here **yesterday**.'	Mary said she had arrived here **yesterday**.
Mary said, 'I'm leaving for Spain **today**.'	Mary said she was leaving for Spain **today**.
Mary said, 'I am leaving for Spain **tomorrow**.'	Mary said she was leaving for Spain **tomorrow**.

If we are reporting the conversation the next day, the changes will be:

Yesterday.	**Today.**
Mary said, 'I arrived here **yesterday**.'	Mary said she had arrived here **the day before**.
Mary said, 'I am leaving for Spain **today**.'	Mary said she was leaving for Spain **yesterday**.
Mary said, 'I'm leaving for Spain **tomorrow**.'	Mary said she was leaving for Spain **today**.

However, once a few days have gone by since the original statement was spoken, changes will occur in the following ways.

Yesterday *will become* **the day before**; **today** *will become* **that day**; *and* **tomorrow** *will become* **the day after** *or* **the next day**.

*Let's look at these senten*ces.

Some days ago.	**Today.**
Mary said, 'I arrived here **yesterday**.'	Mary said she had arrived there **the day before**.
Mary said, 'I'm leaving for Spain **today**.'	Mary said she was leaving for Spain **that day**.
Mary said, 'I'm leaving for Spain **tomorrow**.'	Mary said she was leaving for Spain **the next day**.

And time phrases with **ago** *will change to* **before** *or* **earlier**; **time** *will change to* **later** *and* **next** *will change to* **following**.

Mary said, 'I arrived here two days **ago**.'	Mary said she had arrived here two days **before/earlier**.
Mary said, 'I'm leaving in two days **time**.'	Mary said she was leaving two days **later**.

There are other ways of converting direct time to reported time; for instance, **days** *and* **dates** *might be used. Look at these sentences.*

Mary said, 'Come and see me on **Monday**.'	She told me to come and see her on (the following) **Monday**.
Mary said, 'It's on the **25th of May**.'	She said it was on the **25th of May**.

Modals and semi-modals.

Modals *experience the same time changes as verbs. Their tense is governed by the tense of the reporting verb. Look at these sentences.*

She says, 'I **can't** come today.'	She says she **can't** come today.
Peter is saying, 'I **may** be here.'	He is saying he **may** be here.
They said, 'We **will** be here on time.'	They said they **would** be there on time.
I said, 'I **would** come.'	I said I **would** come.
He asked, '**Could** you come to our party?'	He asked us if we **could** come to their party.
He asked, 'Where **should** I sit?'	He asked where he **should** sit.

Note: Past *modals do not change.*

But*; but* **shall** *does not become* **should**:

She said, 'I **shall** see you tomorrow.' *When converted into indirect speech doesn't correlate with*

She said she **should** see you tomorrow. *As you can see the meaning has changed. Use* **would**.

Semi-modals *are converted into indirect speech in the same way as main verbs are. Look at these sentences.*

Mary said, 'I**'m going to** visit John tonight.'	Mary said she **was going to** visit John that night.
Peter said, 'I **plan to** give a party next week.'	Peter said he **planned to** give a party the following week.
John asked, '**Did** they **want to** leave early?'	John asked if they **had wanted to** leave early.
Jane asked, 'Where **have** you **put** the books?'	Jane asked where he **had put** the books.

And so on.

INVERSION or fronting

Inversions or fronting are more common in the written form and have a formal and, in some cases, a poetic presentation; they are also used to give emphasis or create suspense. They occur when the order of the sentence is reversed. There are two ways in which this is done; the first is the straight forward **subject/verb** *reversal as in closed questions. Look at these sentences.*

He **has** bought some cheese.	**Has** he bought some cheese?
He **can** come tomorrow.	**Can** he come tomorrow?

The second form of inversion is a bit more complicated because it has a variety of forms. Look at these sentences.

Starting with **prepositions**.

The children frolicked among the flowers.	Among the flowers the children frolicked.
His name was on the page.	On the page was his name.
The plane flew into the clouds.	Into the clouds flew the plane.

Starting with **here** *and* **there**.

The man stood there.	There stood the man.
He came here.	Here he came.
She lay on the bed.	There on the bed she lay.

Starting with **having** *implying* **after**.

I left **after** I paid the bill.	Having paid the bill I left.
I left **after** I spoke to her.	Having spoken to her I left.
He had breakfast **after** his shower.	Having had a shower he had breakfast.

And there are others, like:

I **have seldom** seen such beauty.	**Seldom have** I seen such beauty.
They **rarely flower** in the winter.	**Rarely do they flower** in the winter.
He planted the bomb.	**It was he who planted** the bomb.
John told us the good news.	**It was John who told** us the good news.

It's not often you'll find the opportunity to use these structures. But have fun anyway!

PHRASAL VERBS

*Phrasal verbs *are the bane of ESL teachers' lives. We have experienced the difficulties inherent in teaching them. But teach them we must as they are an integral part of informal English.*

*Phrasal verbs *are made up of a* **verb** *and an* **adverb** *or* **preposition***; this combination generally changes the meaning of the main verb. Note the use of* **made up** *in the previous sentence. The verb* ***make*** *usually connotes the production of something as in; She* ***made*** *the cake; but when it is combined with the adverb* **up***, there can be a multiple of meanings. Look at these sentences.*

Peter **made up** the story; it wasn't true.
I needed $100.00 but I had only $75; my brother **made up** the difference.
They **made up** after they realized that they really liked each other.
They kissed and **made up**.

The problem occurs when we look at where to place the object of the sentence with different phrasal verbs. There doesn't appear to be a standard location! In the first two sentences the phrasal verb can be split by the object or a pronoun; however, in the third sentence the phrasal verb cannot be split by a noun or pronoun. The fourth sentence doesn't require an object or completion. One explanation is; some phrasal verbs are prepositional and some are adverbial, go figure! So;

In the first sentence we learn that Peter concocted the story.
In the second sentence we learn that his brother gave him $25.
In the third sentence we learn they are not quarrelling any more.
The succinct fourth sentence states the same as the third sentence.

In sentences three and four the phrasal verb cannot be split; and there is a change in meaning.

So we come to the question; how do we teach **phrasal verbs***?*

I am sure you have your way; I use the following symbols:

[----] = **can't be separated**
[----] [----] = **can be separated**
* = **a noun or pronoun may be used**

^ = a pronoun is not usually used
>< = meaning may change

I encourage my students to use these symbols to remind them of how a particular phrasal verb might be used. I also ask them to make their own phrasal verb dictionary; a small note book will do. They follow these examples.

[look after]* = to take care of / to mind someone or something.
Hospitals **look after** people who are ill.
He **looks after** his shoes well. He **looks after** them.
Don't worry. I'll **look after** your cat while you're away.

[turn]*[on] >< = to start a machine or electronic equipment / to attack / to arouse sexually.
Could you **turn on** the radio?
Could you **turn** it **on**?
.>< The dog **turned on** the snake. (attacked the snake)
>< He was **turned on** by the sex scenes in the movie.

[turn]*[off]^ = opposite action to **turn on** with the exception of the third sentence.

[turn]*[up]*^>< = increase the volume level /appear/arrive (suddenly)
He is always **turning up** the volume.
Why do you keep **turning** it **up**?
>< Mary **turned up** unexpectedly.

Then there are three word phrasal verbs. Which look like this: **verb+adverb+preposition.** *These phrasal verbs are not usually split. Here are some examples.*

[look forward to] = a pleasant expectation
I **look forward to** meeting your parents.
                    visiting your beautiful country.
                    reading your latest book.

[run out of] = use up, finish, empty.(mainly consumables)
We have **run out of** milk; we need to get some more.
Be careful, you might **run out of** time.
They had **run out of** money and had to return home early.

[catch up with] = to make up for lost time, to meet up with old friends, to prevent falling behind.

She had missed two lessons, she decided to stay home and **catch up with** her lessons.

Go ahead; I'll **catch up with** you later.

I'm going down to the cafe to **catch up with** some friends I haven't seen for some time.

[keep up with] = to maintain the same level as others in a variety of things.

You're walking too fast. I can't **keep up with** you.

He found it difficult to **keep up with** his payments. The bank was threatening to foreclose.

Keeping up with the Joneses can cause a lot of anxiety.

QUESTIONS

Part of Speech	Types	Position and function	Form	Example
Questions	There are five ways of asking questions.	Three of which use auxiliary verbs or modals in specific positions. Questions are asked to get information. (The main verb, in most instances, is in its base form). The open questions don't always require an object. Some question words can be followed by a noun.		
	closed	only ask for a 'yes' or 'no' answer; and is used to verify information. The sentence always begins with an auxiliary verb or modal. Semi-modal questions always begin with an auxiliary verb.	**Aux-verb** subject completion? **Aux- verb** subject ~ing-verb completion? **Aux-verb** subject base-verb completion? **Modal** subject base-verb completion? **Aux-verb** subject semi-modal base-verb completion?	**Are** you a teacher? **Is** he playing tennis today? **Do** you live here? **Can** you come early? **Will** she marry him? **Did** he want to go to the cinema tonight?

open	begin with a question word and is usually followed by an auxiliary verb or modal. The exception is when the answer to the question is the subject of the sentence, in which case the **Q word** replaces the subject; the question has the characteristics of a regular sentence. These questions are used to discover information.	**Q word aux-verb** subject ~ing-verb (completion)? **Q word modal** subject base- verb (completion)? **Q word aux-verb** ~ing-verb (completion)? **Q word** verb (completion)? **Q word** c. noun followed by any of the above combinations.	**What are** you doing here at this time of night? **When can** we have dinner tonight? **Who is** playing tennis today on the centre court? **Who** lives here? **Which** book do you want to buy? **What** *nationality* are those students?
tag	are declarative sentences followed by a short question, using an auxiliary verb or modal usually followed by a pronoun. These questions are normally used to confirm information or get agreement. We don't use **amn't** so **aren't** is used instead; however, there are variants such as **am I not?**, **ain't I?** etc., that are accepted in some parts of the English speaking world.	positive sentence, short negative question? negative sentence, short positive question? subject modal base-verb completion, negative modal pronoun? subject negative aux or modal base-verb, positive aux or modal pronoun?	Peter **is** a teacher, **isn't** he? They **live** here, **don't** they? They **aren't** happy, are they? They don't live here, do they? They **can** sing, **can't** they? You **will** come to the party, **won't** you? He **isn't** a teacher, **is** he? They **can't** come, **can** they? **I'm** a teacher, **aren't** I?

indirect	are a combination of closed questions and any other questions; both closed and open. **If** or **Q words** are used in the form of conjunctions.	closed question **if** subject verb completion? closed question **Q word** subject verb completion?	Do you know **if** tomorrow is a holiday? Can you tell me **where** I can buy a bus ticket?
voiced	are formed by raising the voice as one gets to the end of the sentence. These are usually used to express surprise or disbelief.	Positive sentence? ↗ Negative sentence?	You are a teacher? ↗ You don't like ice cream?

Looking at these five ways of asking questions in more detail. To recap.

type	structure	purpose
closed	always begin with an auxiliary verb or modal.	to check information.
open	always begin with a question word then is followed by an auxiliary verb or modal or noun.	to seek information.
tag	statement followed by short opposing question.	to seek confirmation.
indirect	closed question followed by statement.	polite form.
voiced	statement spoken in rising intonation.	to show surprise or disbelief.

Let's look at each type.

CLOSED QUESTIONS.

Closed questions are so called because they have only two answers: **'Yes'** *or* **'No'**.

As we have seen under **Auxiliary verbs**, *there are three types of auxiliary verbs; be-verbs, 'invisible (dummy) verbs' and perfect verbs.*

The be-verbs are: **am**, **is**, **are**, **was**, **were**.
The 'invisible' verbs are: **do**, **does**, **did**.
The perfect verbs are: **have**, **has**, **had**.

Be-verbs:

In the sentence form, the be-verb is the main verb; to form a closed question the main verb is put in the beginning of the sentence, thus:

You **are** a teacher.	**Are** you a teacher?
That **is** your book.	**Is** that your book?
I **am** learning English.	**Am** I learning English?/**Are** you learning English?
They **were** playing football.	**Were** they playing football?

'Invisible' verbs: sometimes referred to as the 'dummy' verb!

Unlike the be-verbs, the main verb is not placed at the beginning of the sentence to form the question; instead the auxiliary verbs **Do**, **Does**, *or* **Did** *is placed at the beginning of the sentence and the main verb takes on the base form. Thus:*

I do my homework after dinner.	**Do** I do my homework after dinner?
She plays the piano after school.	**Does** she play the piano after school?

I had a good meal last night.   **Did** you have a good meal last night?

Perfect:

Here the 3rd//past participle of the verb is added to **have**, **has**, **had**; *thus:*

I **have** visited Hong Kong.   **Have** you visited Hong Kong?

They **have** bought a new house.   **Have** they bought a new house?

I **had** seen that film.   **Had** you/I seen that film?

Modal questions.

Modal questions are similar to the perfect questions, in that, the modal is contained in the main sentence, and to form the question the modals are transferred to the beginning of the sentence. Remember, modals are always accompanied by base verb, giving us the following forms:

Mary **can** sing.   **Can** Mary sing?

It **will** rain tomorrow.   **Will** it rain tomorrow?

You **should** see a doctor. **Should** I see a doctor?

Questions may be asked in the negative form; however, these questions may suggest disbelief, surprise, incredulity or seek confirmation.

Aren't you a teacher?	Suggests that you were expected to be a teacher.
Weren't you at the party?	Suggests that you were expected to be at the party.
Isn't she beautiful?	The speaker thinks she's beautiful and seeks confirmation.
Wasn't the movie great?	The speaker thinks the movie was very good and seeks confirmation or agreement.

OPEN QUESTIONS.

Open questions are so called because one question can have as many answers as are possible. Take the question; **What's your name?** *The answer to this question can be as many as there are people on the earth!*

Open questions can cause problems to learners of English because they usually contain auxiliary verbs or modal, which not all languages use when asking open questions.

Each utterance contains several pieces of information; each piece of information can generate a question.

'I am a student' *can generate two questions, because there are two pieces of information contained in the sentence; the subject,* **I,** *and the object,* **a student.** *When the* **subject** *of the sentence is expected to be the* **answer** *to the question we merely replace the* **subject** *with the question words* **Who** *or* **What.** *Hence:*

subject		verb	completion	
1. The woman	**2.** near the window	**3.** won	**4.** a gold medal	**5.** at the Olympics.

('The woman sitting by the window **[subject]**) won **[verb]** (a gold medal at the last Olympics.' **[completion]**).
'The woman sitting by the window' *is the answer we want, so the question will be;*
Who won a gold medal at the last Olympics?
Let's look further: the sentence has four pieces of information.

1.   *woman* near the window **[subject]**

2.   near the window **[place]**

3.   won (a gold medal) **[verb]**

4.   a gold medal **[1ˢᵗ object]**

5.   at the last Olympics. **(2ⁿᵈ object [when/where [{completion}])**

So we can ask four questions. We have already asked the first question, so we can go on to:

1.   **Where** is the woman sitting?

2.   *When the answer required is the verb of the sentence, the question always contains a version of the verb* **'do'** *depending on the tense of the sentence. In this example the tense is in the past simple so the question will be in the past simple: The question word will always be* **What.**
     What did the woman sitting by the window **do**?

3.   **What did** the woman (sitting by the window) **win**?

4.   **When/Where did** she **win** it?

I use a number chart to illustrate open questions; like this: The method is a bit contrived, but it seems to work.

subject		verb	completion	
1. The woman	**2.** near the window	**3.** won	**4.** a gold medal	**5.** at the Olympics

Question forming 1.

	Q word	aux				answers
1	**Who**		**3**	**4**	**5?**	**The woman** near the window.
2	**Where**	was	**1?**			**near the window.**
3	**what**	did	**1**	do?		**won** a gold medal.
4	**What**	did	**1**	win?		**a gold medal.**
5	**When/Where**	did	**1**	win	**4?**	**at the Olympics.**

Let's look at another sentence.

1. Peter	**2.** is **2a.** taking	**3.** Mary	**4.** to the cinema	**5.** tonight	**6.** by bus.

Question forming 2.

	Q word	aux					answers
1	**Who**	**2/2a**		**3**	**4**	**5**	**6?**	**Peter.**
2	**What**	is	**1**	doing with		**3**	**5?**	**taking** her to the cinema.
3	**Who(m)**	is	**1**	**2a**	**4**	**5?**		**Mary.**
4	**Where**	is	**1**	**2a**	**3**	**5?**		**to the cinema.**
5	**When**	is	**1**	**2a**	**3**	**4?**		**tonight.**
6	**How**	is	**1**	**2a**	**3**	**4**	**5?**	**by bus.**

This can be done with all kinds of sentences.

Open questions need careful and continuous practice to prevent students from reverting to first language structures. Also asking accurately for information will help get accurate answers.

What, **Whose** *and* **Which** *can also have common nouns placed after them; These questions are enquiring after the common nouns. Look at these sentences.*

What book *did you buy?*
Which book *did you buy?*
Whose car *is parked in the driveway?*

The enquirer wants to know some more about the **book** *and the* **car.**

TAG QUESTIONS.

Questions asked in the tag form are, in a way, persuasive questions, seeking to get agreement or confirmation from the listener.
They are formed in two ways. A positive statement accompanied by a short negative question or a negative statement accompanied by a short positive question. The question segment is made up of an auxiliary verb or modal and a subject pronoun. The auxiliary verb or modal in the question segment matches that contained in the main sentence. The questions are meant to elicit agreement. Look at these sentences.

I**'m** in time for class, **aren't** I? (remember, we don't use **amn't**)
They **are**n't students, **are** they?
We **can** leave now, **can**'t we?
You **have** seen that film, **have**n't you?

and so on.

Today **is** Monday, isn't it? **Yes, it is.**
They **aren't** students, are they? **No, they aren't.**

Affirmative information can be responded to with a short negative question to indicate agreement. Look at these sentences.

'She's a lovely person.'	Reply: '**Isn't she!**'
'She looked beautiful.'	Reply: '**Didn't she!**'

They might also suggest enthusiastic agreement.

'She's a lovely person'	Reply: '**Isn't she!**'

Note: *The tense of the short question matches the tense of the sentence it is responding to.*

INDIRECT QUESTIONS.

Indirect questions soften the question. They give the listener time to prepare themselves for the question. They are formed in two ways; **closed** *question plus* **closed** *question and* **closed** *question plus* **open** *question. When making a* **closed** *plus* **closed** *question, the connector is* **if***; when making a* **closed** *plus* **open** *question the connector is the* **question word** *of the open question. The most common indirect questions are shown in the chart. The format is as below:*

indirect question	connector	subject	verb	completion? (if required)
Do you know **Do you have any idea** **Can you tell me** **Could you tell me**	if what who when where etc.	he the shop I the man in blue Mary etc.	is coming to opens? is? can find plays etc.	school? the party? football? a shoe shop? his way here? etc.

Here are some indirect questions:

Do you know **if** he is coming to school?
Do you have any idea **where** the shop is?
Can you tell me **when** the banks open?
Can you tell him **when** he can play football?

As you can see, after the connector the sentence is no longer a question but a declarative sentence. Other sentences using this type of format are: (the subject and tense may vary)

I*don't know
I can't remember I wonder
I would like to know

*The relevant subject is used. Remember the tense of the first verb affects the tense of subsequent verbs. Look at these sentences.

	connector	subject	verb	completion
He doesn't know **Mary is wondering** **They would like to know** **Peter couldn't* remember**	where if when where what etc.	his teacher you he the shop they the students etc.	lives. will leave. is coming would like want to go. had etc.	home. for breakfast. etc.

*most modals can be used.

Here are some indirect sentences.

He doesn't know **where** his teacher lives.
Mary is wondering **if** he is coming for breakfast.
Peter couldn't remember **what** his teacher's name was.

ASKING QUESTIONS WITH 'HOW'.

	adjective	auxiliary verb	subject	completion	
How	far, tall, long, fast, expensive, etc.	am, is, are, was, were.	I your son? Queen St the dinner, etc.	from here? last night? etc.	

	frequency	auxiliary verb	subject	base verb	completion
How	often, frequently	do, does, did.	the bus, you, Peter, the girls, etc.	come? eat play etc.	out? tennis? etc.

	frequency	auxiliary verb	subject	3rd participle	completion
How	often frequently	have, has, had.	John, he, the boys, you, etc.	played eaten driven etc.	tennis? out? a truck? etc.

	frequency	modals	subject	base verb	completion
How	often frequently	will, would, can, could, should, etc.	they, she, you, etc.	stay go buy etc.	there? abroad? cheese? etc.

	quantity	plural common nouns	auxiliary verbs	subject	verbs
How	many	cars, cats, people, books, movies, etc.	are, were, do, did, have, had **modals** will, would, can, could, etc.	there (here)? you, they, we, people, John, etc.	see? seen? taken? **base verbs** buy? take? etc.

	quantity	uncountable common nouns	auxiliary verbs	subject	verbs
How	much	water, cheese, sugar, hydrogen, etc.	is, was, does, did, has, had **modals as above**	as above	as above

Looks a bit confusing at first glance, but you should be able to work it out. These sample sentences should help you make sense of the charts.

How far is the bus stop from here?
How many people can you see?
How much cheese did you buy?
How often does Peter play tennis?
How frequently do you eat in a restaurant?
How much cheese can we buy for $25.00?
How expensive was the train trip across Canada?

RELATIVE CLAUSES

Relative *clauses are sentences that follow the relative* **pronouns**. *There are two types of* **Relative** *clauses;* **defining** *and* **non-defining**. **Defining** *clauses are necessary to clarify the person or thing referred to in the sentence; without which there might be some ambiguity;* **non- defining** *clauses are purely informative, adding a tit-bit of interest to the sentence and is contained within commas. This information can be easily omitted without altering the main meaning of the sentence.*

I like to explain the **defining** *clause as verbal finger-pointing. If I ask,* **'Who is that person?'** *– to pin point the person I am referring to, I would need to point* **at** *the person, which could be embarrassing. In this situation I need an indicator as to whom I am referring to; so I would ask, 'Who is that person* **(who is) standing by the door?'** *The clause* **'who is standing by the door'** *'points' to the person I am referring to. No embarrassment caused!* **Defining** *clauses are generally used with common (concrete) nouns.*

Non-defining *clauses can be used with words that are self-explanatory; such as proper nouns (names) and common nouns that are defined by possessive or demonstrative pronouns. Look at these sentences.*

Toyotas which are made in Japan are reliable cars.
The car which I bought yesterday is a Toyota.
My car which I bought yesterday is a Toyota.
This car which is a rental has seen a lot of mileage.

In the first sentence 'Toyotas' is an identifiable trade name and requires no further identification so the sentence that follows the relative pronoun **which** *is not really necessary; so it should be enclosed with comma;* **Toyotas, which are made in Japan, are reliable cars**. *The sentence could read* **'Toyotas are reliable cars'** *without causing any loss of meaning. We'll ignore other nuances.*

In the second sentence 'The car' could refer to any car; without the **defining** *clause the sentence would read;* **'The car is a Toyota'**. *The information is ambiguous since we don't know* **which** *car. However, once the defining clause is added the car becomes specific and because the clause is strongly related to the 'car', no commas are used.*

In the third and fourth sentences, the possessive pronoun 'My' and the demonstrative pronoun 'This' define the car, so no defining clause is necessary, hence the non-defining clauses included in the sentences only serves an informative purpose; the clauses can be removed without causing any ambiguity. The second sentence should read; 'My car, which I bought yesterday, is a Toyota'. Without the relative clause it would read; 'My car is a Toyota'. There is no ambiguity in this sentence. The third sentence should read; 'This car, which is a rental, has seen a lot of mileage.' Removing the relative clause from this sentence would cause no ambiguity either. The relative clauses can be in any tense, depending on what needs to be said. Let's look at some Relative clauses.

Defining clauses.

The organist **who featured in yesterday's programme** was from Notre Dame. I'm sending a Thank You card to the person **who changed the tyre on my car.**

They are going to give $100 to anyone **who finds their cat.**

The man **whom she married** is an engineer.

The man *to* **whom she is married** is an engineer.

The man **whom she is married** *to* is an engineer.

The house **that is at the end of the street** was sold for a million dollars.

The car **that is parked in front of my house** has been there for two days.

The woman **whose husband died a few months ago** has inherited a lot of money.

He gave me **what I asked for.**

They did **what was wanted.**

I'll see you in the evening **when you are at home.**

There was a time **when she was happy.**

They always meet at the same place **where the rooms are very comfortable.**

She had a good reason **why she couldn't come.**

The reason **why I didn't come** is none of your business.

Non-defining clauses.

Peter, **who is a maths teacher,** went on holiday last week.

My neighbours, **who all work for Air New Zealand,** keep different hours.

She was waiting for her boyfriend *for* **whom she had bought a scarf.**

He was looking at a photograph of his wife, **whom he was separated** *from.*

Queen Street, **which is Auckland's main street**, is very busy at the weekends.

Great Expectations, **that was written almost 200 years ago,** is still very popular.

Anthony Smith, **whose house is behind those trees,** is away in the Caribbean.

We go on holiday in June, **when the weather is hot.**

I'm going to Cuba again, **where the people are wonderful.**

Put the keys on my table, **where I can see them.**

Truncated relative sentences.

A relative clause can be shortened when the clause contains **who**, **that** *or* **which**. *There are three ways of shortening relative clauses. Look at these examples:*

1. *In some instances we can just omit the relative pronoun;* **who**, **that** *or* **which**. *So in 'The* book **which** I bought yesterday has pages missing.';* **which** *can be removed without loss of meaning;* 'The book I bought yesterday has pages missing.'

2. 'The woman **who is** wearing the red dress is a famous singer' *can be shortened to:* 'The woman **wearing** the red dress is a famous singer.' *This type of sentence is referred to as an adjectival phrase.*

3. *In this sentence;* 'All those **who plan** to take the exam should wait after class';* *there is no* **be- verb** *after* **who** *so when we omit* **who** *the verb* **plan** *takes on the* —ing *form;* **planning**. *So the sentence changes to:* 'All those **planning** to take the exam should wait after class.'

Look at these sentences: The crossed out words can be omitted without a loss of meaning.

1. The road ~~that~~ Peter lives on has very old trees.

   The person ~~whom~~ she married turned out to be a rogue.
   The photo ~~which~~ Mary sent to the newspaper won her $500.00

2. The car ~~that is~~ parked in the driveway is blocking my car.

   The car ~~that is parked~~ in the driveway is blocking my car.
   The people ~~who are~~ walking up the road are protesting.
   The books ~~that were~~ written by Steinbeck are still very popular.

*The following sentences contain no be-verbs and so change is twofold;
nevertheless, there is no change in meaning.*

3.   In the southern hemisphere, houses that face north get more sun.
     Change one; delete **that;** *change two; change the verb* **face** *to the
     gerund* **facing.**

     The sentence can now be; 'In the southern hemisphere, houses **facing**
     north get more sun.'

Most people ~~who~~ visit Spain want to watch a bullfight.
becomes
Most people **visiting** Spain want to watch a bullfight.

Students ~~who~~ come to school by bus can have tomorrow off.
becomes
Students **coming** to school by bus can have tomorrow off.

And so on.

TWO Ts OR NOT TWO Ts

*There's a simple rule for repeating the last letter of a word when extending
it. The repetition of the last letter, usually a consonant, depends on the
length of the vowel sound before or around it. When there is a long vowel
sound, the last letter is not repeated. So* **dine** *(say it) which has a* **long**
vowel sound becomes **diner;** *but* **din** *(say it) which has a* **short** *vowel sound
becomes* **dinner.** *Another way to look at it is; if the word ends with a* **vowel/
consonant/vowel** *combination the last letter is not repeated.*

*But don't rely too heavily on this rule — exceptions lurk around every
linguistic corner.*
*I before E except after C – Yeah, right! --- atheism, beige, caffeine, heir,
seize, etc, etc ...*

PART 5
Exercises

EXERCISES

It is suggested that these exercises be done in pairs or groups; after all, language is a communicative tool and students working on their own are certainly not communicating. Projecting the exercises on the board using OHPs or a computer would be an ideal way to encourage group participation.

Often when students are working together they reach a point where they cannot discuss the exercise they are doing in the target language and they are forced to resort to other means. The two most common methods are; using the electronic language devices that are now available and most students have; and discussing the problem with other students, sometimes in their first language. Given this situation I would rather have students discussing the problem in their own language than looking up the solution in their electronic devices. The discussion generates a better understanding of the problem they are having with the exercise; whereas, the device merely provides them with an expedient solution.

My criticism of most exercises in prevailing textbooks is that they do not challenge the learner to solve the more intricate nature of language. In gapfill exercises often all that is required is to put in one word and a clue is often provided at the end of the sentence. The student, on completing these exercises, often only focuses on the gap that needs to be filled and pays scant attention to the rest of the sentence. At the more advanced level there might be a clause or phrase that might need to be inserted, but once again there are clues provided. Scrambled sentences contain all the words to re-form the sentence which, again, is no challenge. The learner merely has to puts them in the right order; often simply numbering the words rather than writing them out into the correct, complete sentence. So what we get is something like this:

4	3	5	2	1
New York	for	yesterday	left	Peter

In matching two halves of a sentence, the student merely draws a line from one half to the other in their textbooks - the exercises ends up looking like a complex drawing of roadways.

Some of my exercises require the student to notice that a word is missing and then to fill the gap with the appropriate word or words.

*The students are not going to get **every** sentence right (some are quite complex), but in endeavouring to get them right, I hope they will have got a better understanding of how English works.*

Remember, this is a collaborative effort, teacher and students should work together to work out the difficult exercises. The teacher encouraging the students towards the solution, constantly referring back to the relevant lesson.

Encourage students to work with the whole sentence by asking them to write the complete sentence in their notebook rather than just putting in the required word. I have seen students write the one word in their notebook; how they are going to relate it to the original sentence - Who knows!

EXERCISES
ADJECTIVES
Base, comparatives and superlatives.

Put the correct form of the base verbs provided in the box into the correct sentence. There are a few extra words. Fact is not essential.

brown	danger	fast	happy	old	blue	angry	hot	good	clear	favourite
large	expensive		handsome	poor	interest	rich	energy	tire	wet	red

Look at the example.

She speaks a_____language.
She speaks a foreign language.

Now you try.

1. She doesn't look_____, what do you think is the problem?

2. Janet has_____eyes, but her sister has_____eyes.

3. Phew! It's_____in here, could you open the window?

4. The_____plane (NASA X-43A) travelled at 7,460 mph.

5. The Caspian Sea is_____the Dead Sea.

6. Which is_____restaurant in the world?

7. Cynthia got very_____when she missed her train.

8. Matthew is very_____, but he refuses to work as a model.

9. The sky is_____, I don't think it's going to rain.

10. Bangladesh is probably_____country in the world.

11. The city of Port Moresby is_____than Chicago.

12. Football_____as rugby.

13. What is your_____colour?

14. The dinner smells very_____.

15. It is thought that Damascus in Syria is_____city in the world.

EXERCISES
Unscramble the sentences and use the words in the box in their correct form. Some changes may be necessary. Facts are not essential.

lovely	similar	hungry	tall	clever	different	interesting	same	new
heavy	friendly	expensive	polite	easy	fast	exciting	rich	fun	popular

Look at the example.

Margaret in the is student class.
Margaret is **the*** **cleverest** *student in the class.*
necessary for superlative adjectives.

Now you try.

1. brother as Mary as isn't her.

2. building you world know which is in Do the?

3. The are the from very Chinese Koreans.

4. I apple feel, I have I'll an think.

5. I shirt colour the as yours a have.

6. mine baby Her is.

7. know She he and a is person I.

8. cats are Dogs.

9. she dress is mine wearing is The.

10. shoes planning pair to very buy a of I'm.

11. world Paul Getty to man in be used the.

12. looked dress She in wonderful that.

13. one last This was test the.

14. It eaten meal ever had was I.

15. is school the student Jennifer in.

EXERCISES
~ed adjectives
Put the right adjective in its correct form in the correct sentence.

| disappoint | exhaust | depress | excite | interest | amaze | amuse | astonish |
| surprise | bore | annoy | disgust | impress | terrify | embarrass | shock |

Look at the example.

Peter's been very_____since his girlfriend left him.
*Peter has been very depress**ed** since his girlfriend left him.*

Now you try.
1. We were all_____by the news of his sudden death.

2. Some people are_____at the thought of eating chicken feet.

3. I'm_____I think I'll go home early.

4. Everyone was_____when they heard she had climbed Everest alone.

5. He always works very hard, I am not_____he is doing so well.

6. I don't go to his lectures; I'm not_____in what he says.

7. I'm so_____about my trip to the Amazon.

8. We all were_____by the last fight between Frazier and Muhammad Ali.

9. I was quite_____by all the mistakes I had made.

10. He gets really_____by all the bad news in the media.

11. I'm_____by how some people can learn languages so naturally.

12. I was_____when I thought the car was going to hit the tree.

13. Peter has a very good sense of humour; we are_____by his stories.

14. We were_____by the quality of the food in that restaurant.

15. Intelligent people should never get_____.

EXERCISES
~ing adjectives
Put the right adjective in its correct form in the correct sentence.

disappoint	exhaust	depress	excite	interest	amaze	amuse	innovate
surprise	bore	annoy	disgust	confuse	terrify	embarrass	shock

Look at the example.

His exam results were very_____.
*His exam results were very disappoint**ing**.*

Now you try.

1. The marathon is a very_____race.

2. Sometimes the lessons can be quite_____.

3. His habit of tapping his pencil on the table is quite_____.

4. To say the wrong thing can be_____.

5. Mathematics can be an_____subject.

6. This book was_____it made me very sad.

7. I am not sure I want an_____life.

8. Dali was an_____artist.

9. I heard a very   story yesterday.

10. That was quite a_____accident we saw yesterday.

11. The movie had a_____end.

12. Finding a body in the boot of the car was_____.

13. He told us a very_____story.

14. Very few things are_____to me.

15. Spitting on the street is a very_____habit.

EXERCISES
3rd/past participles (irregular verbs)
Put the right adjective in the appropriate sentence.

stolen	well-made	home-made	self-taught	beaten	mislaid	bought	torn	
frozen	hidden	hand-written	discarded	half-eaten	lost	cut	broken	recycled

Look at the example.

The police found the_____bicycle.
*The police found the **stolen** bicycle.*

Now you try.

1. You don't often see a_____-_____letter these days.
2. The_____city of Troy was found 200 years ago.
3. _____cakes are not as good as_____-_____cakes.
4. _____vegetables are no different from fresh vegetables.
5. His house is full of_____furniture.
6. The_____letter was never found.
7. I took my_____coat to the tailor to have it mended.
8. The_____team was very disappointed at its loss.
9. We put all the_____glass in the recycle bin.
10. Peter always wears_____-_____suits.
11. Who left this_____-_____apple on the table?
12. The boy showed his_____little finger to his mother.
13. The painting was well-_____no one knew where it was.
14. There are a lot of_____items found on the bus.
15. John speaks German very well, even though he is_____-_____.

EXERCISES
ADJECTIVE ORDER: Now put these adjectives into the right column in the chart below to describe the nouns.

tall	damaged	soft	lengthy	written	success	Thai	successful	gorgeous	brown	nylon	fur	thick	thin	slim
fat	enormous	bald	light	striped	shy	frightened	polite	rude	friendly	neat	next	empty	full	cold
wintry	windy	different	same	hungry	simple	lucky	sad	miserable	expensive	red	cheap	swollen	quick
excellent	bad	delicious	good	tasty	perfect	best	Japanese	cosy	exciting	dull	colourful	cheap	rich

	1 word	2 words	3 words	4 words	5 words	6 words	7 words	8 words	9 words
shoes	*red*								
flat									
bird									
family									
woman									
jacket									
restaurant									
child									
city									

The first one has been done for you.

EXERCISES
Use the words in brackets in their right form and in the correct position.
Proper nouns have been underlined.

Look at the example.
The food was; we couldn't eat it. *(disgust)*
*The food was **disgusting**; we couldn't eat it.*

Now you try.

1.   The <u>Bentley</u> is an car. *(expensive)*

2.   The <u>Sky Tower</u> is the <u>ASB</u> building. *(high)*

3.   Could you suggest an novel. *(excite)*

4.   He gave us a very explanation. *(interest)*

5.   <u>Hemingway</u> wrote several novels. *(drama)*

6.   The blue whale is an elephant. *(large)*

7.   I bought a _, _, _ shirt. **(use any three adjectives)**

8.   Some people think <u>Steinbeck</u> is a writer <u>Hemingway</u>. *(good)*

9.   Who is that man by the door? *(stand)*

10. The police are looking for the painting. *(steal)*

11. Some people think the <u>Mona Lisa</u> is picture ever painted. *(great)*

12. <u>Tokyo</u> is <u>Hong Kong</u>. *(populate)*

13. Are you she can't come to the party? *(sure)*

14. <u>John</u> looks so; he must have failed his exam. *(depress)*

15. That was a very offer; I had to accept it. *(generous)*

EXERCISES
Adjectival SUFFIXES
Put the correct form of the adjective in the gap provided. Some changes might be necessary.

Verbs & nouns

grace	motion change	price	enjoy	romance	sleep	forget power	truth danger
bump			horror	drama	act	care	

Suffixes

~ful	~less ~ive	~able	~tic ~y	~al	~ous	~fic ~ible

Look at the example.

We had a lovely weekend; it was thoroughly_____.
*We had a lovely weekend; it was thoroughly **enjoyable**.*

Now you try.

1. Peter is very_____; he never remembers his appointments.

2. The food wasn't very good, but the restaurant was quite_____.

3. She's a very_____dancer.

4. English is more often spoken in the_____form.

5. The road was very_____; he had to drive very slowly.

6. People feel_____in a non-democratic country.

7. There was an_____accident in the coal mine.

8. His English is good but he tends to make_____mistakes.

9. Because New Zealand is narrow, the weather is very_____.

10. She told the story in a very_____way.

11. *Romeo and Juliet* is probably the most_____story ever written.

12. There was no wind so the boat sat_____on the sea.

13. I wouldn't believe what he says; he finds it very difficult to be_____.

14. I feel very_____; I think I'll go to bed now.

15. Skydiving is a_____activity.

EXERCISES
ADVERBS
Put an appropriate adverb from the box in the right sentence. Some sentences might need an adverb of degree as well.

softly	very	home	eagerly	too	never	quite	unfortunately	8.00 pm	friendly
[I was a child]	hot	carefully	personally	[they came here]		[two days ago]		[hardly ever]	
			normally	[the last decade]	seriously	sometimes			

Look at the example.

_____, people are caring.

Generally, _people are caring._

Now you try.

1. _____, I don't get along with people who smoke.

2. This restaurant_____serves fish for breakfast.

3. These students arrived here_____.

4. My teacher speaks_____to us.

5. The movie starts at_____.

6. I lived with my grandparents when_____.

7. This coffee is_____, I can't drink it yet.

8. _____, Peter lost his job.

9. Some of the exercises were_____difficult.

10. They all went_____to watch the parade.

11. They were living in Hong Kong before_____.

12. They_____go to the library.

13. That chair is_____comfortable.

14. New Zealand had some interesting changes in_____.

15. The trainer spoke_____and calmly to the horse.

EXERCISES
Complete the sentences with an appropriate adverb or adverbial phrase. There are vast possibilities!

Look at the example.

John has been dating Mary since_____.
John has been dating Mary for_____.
*John has been dating Mary since **they were teenagers.**/since **they met at university.**/for **three years.**/for **some time now.***

Now you try

1. The students' English is getting better.

2. The Smiths haven't left the country.

3. Where will you be?

4. , he was a teacher.

5. Is there you would like to go?

6. I'm really happy. I've bought a house.

7. Have you touched a snake?

8. She is having her party on December.

9. , the sky began to cloud over.

10. I couldn't sing very well before.

11. Since, my English has improved.

12. When they heard the noise, they left.

13. Henry's birthday's on.

14. I can't see you, I have to go to Hamilton.

15. My neighbours have been living here.

EXERCISE
Unscramble these sentences and put in an appropriate adverb or adverbial phrase.

Look at the example.

children the The programme watched.
*The children watched the programme **quietly**.*

Now you try.

1. your coffee here have Do you ?

2. hot Sahara The can Desert get.

3. progress has rapid Electronic made technology.

4. bus things are on leaving People behind the.

5. you No've thank. some I had.

6. stamps I collecting started.

7. on We Tuesdays don't classes have.

8. visit your do you parents How?

9. written has Jack books?

10. drink coffee don't I.

11. car bought Have that you?

12. house they same Are the living in?

13. had rest weather hot The to got for, I stop a.

14. I to movies the go.

15. talks It's difficult to her; she hear too.

EXERCISES
ARTICLES
Put in the missing article. In some sentences you could use 'some'. Some sentences might not need an article.

Look at the example.

Could you pass_____sugar, please?
*Could you pass **the** sugar, please?*

Now you try.

1.   There are stars in_____sky, but you can't see them during_____day.

2.   Did you enjoy_____picnic yesterday.

3.   _____NZ dollar is about 82¢ U.S. at_____moment.

4.   After____heavy rain____sun came out, but there are still ____clouds in_____sky.

5.   I like watching_____baseball; I went to_____game last week.

6.   _____piano isn't_____easy instrument to play well.

7.   _____countries don't have_____one dollar bill.

8.   Did you accept_____excuse John gave for being late?

9.   I saw____accident between____car and____bicycle;____accident was at corner of____Queen St and_____K' Rd.

10. _____Mona Lisa is_____most admired painting in_____world.

11. I can't find____keys to____car. Do you know where____they are?

12. I saw_____birds. They were sitting on_____fence.

13. Euro dollar is worth about_____NZ$2.00.

14. He gave_____unacceptable_____excuse for being late.

15. I had_____chicken and_____rice for dinner._____chicken was_____delicious, but____rice was_____dry.

EXERCISES
Put the articles in these sentences; you might also need to use 'some'.
There are no spaces provided so you'll have to find where to put them.

Look at the example.

I'm very happy with results of test.
*I'm very happy with **the** results of **the** test.*

Now you try.

1. In United States, baseball is very popular sport. To play it you need bat and ball.
2. He gave talk about very interesting book; it was historical novel.
3. I didn't hear announcement about time change and missed train.
4. Don't worry. I'll answer phone if anyone rings.
5. She has longest hair in class.
6. plane was delayed by storm.
7. birds were sitting in tree.
8. For party, I bought wine and cheese; wine was Pinot Noir and cheese was Camembert.
9. police came to house as soon as they could.
10. Why aren't children playing in garden?
11. weather promises to be good on wedding day.
12. mother gave baby wonderful smile.
13. hotel didn't have iron so I had to wear my creased suit.
14. students were encouraged to go to cinema once week.
15. They couldn't pay bill at restaurant; they didn't have enough money.

EXERCISES
Unscramble these sentences and put in the articles or 'some' in the right place.

Look at the example.

trees parks have very Auckland old.
*(The) Auckland parks have **some** very old trees.*

Now you try.

1. tomorrow you office come early in to Could morning?

2. hang clock painting under Don't.

3. best is one in of world Harvard universities.

4. I cinema waited come for but for hour at hotel, her she went didn't so I to.

5. illegal and of problem selling buying is drugs universal.

6. Everest mountain highest in world is.

7. in it boys okay out Is for to go play and park?

8. MR2 I around university, I was drove student in When.

9. States River river Missouri is in longest United.

10. please you butter Can pass?

11. school didn't to learn She play was when she piano child at.

12. war Most at world in of 1940s was.

13. think don't work II put pass can enough test, I haven't in.

14. European around They countryside for drove looking hotel.

15. North Island Mount Ruapehu in is mountain highest.

EXERCISES

a (/ei/), an (/æn/), 'thuh'(/ðə/) or 'thee'(/ði:/)

Write *a* or *an* in the spaces.   **(spoken) Now put *'thuh'* (/ðə/) or
'thee' (/ði:/).**

Look at the examples.

1	.... *a* ....BBC programme	*thuh(/ðə/)*
2	.... *an* ....elephant enclosure	*thee(/ði:/)*

Now you try.

3	.............eucalyptus tree	
4	.............Euro coin	
5	.............European country	
6	.............happy girl	
7	.............H-bomb	
8	.............honest dollar	
9	.............honorable man	
10	....hospice patient	
11	.............hospital	
12	.............hotel car park	
13	.............hour later	
14	.............L-shaped room	
15	.............MD	
16	.............Medical officer	
17	.............MG car	
18	.............MI6 officer	
19	.............NZ dollar	
20	.............New Zealand $	
21	.............one dollar bill	
22	.............T-shirt	
23	.............UFO sighting	
24	.............UNESCO worker	
25	.............unit of work	
26	.............united people	
27	.............universal problem	
28	.............university student	
29	.............unreasonable decision	
20	.............X-ray	

EXERCISES
AUXILIARY VERBS

Put the correct auxiliary verb in these sentences. Look at the example.

They_____students.

*They **are** students.*

Now you try.

1. _____they students?

2. He_____n't an engineer.

3. _____they coming to the party?

4. The students_____late for class.

5. _____you play tennis?

6. Who_____you talking to at the party last night?

7. I_____n't seen that film yet.

8. _____they leave early last night?

9. The girls_____coming here tomorrow.

10. What book_____you read last week?

11. They_____finished their housework.

12. How many books_____you read this month?

13. She_____drink tea.

14. They_____bought some interesting pictures.

15. _____they leaving soon?

EXERCISES
Put the correct auxiliary verb in the right place.

Look at the example.

He lost his keys somewhere.
*He **has** lost his keys somewhere.*

Now you try.

1. How much the computer cost?
2. What you do last night?
3. you do your homework after dinner?
4. She do the housework last night.
5. Peter eaten any breakfast today.
6. They going shopping tomorrow afternoon.
7. He like to play tennis.
8. Jane walking to the shop when she lost her money.
9. they already left for Brussels?
10. Where you planning to go next week?
11. Who she finally marry?
12. The children quite happy with their presents.
13. the police arrive before he got home?
14. Her friend buy the house.
15. Harry become a lawyer.

EXERCISES
Unscramble these sentences and put in the correct auxiliary verb.

Look at the example.

buy looking house for Jonathan a to.
*Jonathan **is** looking for a house to buy.*

Now you try.

1. breakfast just I had.

2. doing homework their They.

3. red She dress wearing a.

4. touched snake ever you a?

5. wife London met in Harold living when he his.

6. Paris he train the take to?

7. China never Sally to been.

8. he by window the sitting?

9. bike stolen Somebody my.

10. that buying they of car thinking?

11. restaurant good you for a looking?

12. house sun left when shining I The the.

13. He he too fast the driving when tree hit.

14. evenings do What the you in?

15. living What for do a she?

EXERCISES
CONDITIONALS
Zero and First conditionals.

Put in the correct verb form.

Look at the example.

If it rains this weekend, I_____at home.
If it rains this weekend, I'll stay at home.

Now you try.

1. If I have nothing to do, I_____to the library.

2. When it doesn't rain, I_____for a run.

3. Sandra always answers her email if she_____in the office.

4. The picnic will be cancelled if it_____.

5. Ask Peter to wait for me if he_____.

6. Whenever I phone my ex-wife, she_____me to dinner.

7. If I get a chance to go to Paris, I_____the Louvre.

8. I see a doctor if I_____well.

9. The light_____on when you walk into the room.

10. I phone home if I_____be late.

11. Ice_____if you put it in warm water.

12. If you miss the bus,_____for the next one.

13. When I_____home from work, I always have a wash.

14. If you heat water to a 100°, it_____.

15. If you get caught in the rain,_____shelter.

EXERCISES
Zero and First conditionals.

Choose the correct alternative.

Look at the example.

If it rains this weekend, *I stay at home./I'll stay at home.*
If it rains this weekend, **I'll stay at home.**

Now you try.

1. If you speak slowly, *they may understand you./they are going to understood you.*

2. When I read, *I wear my glasses./I will wear my glasses.*

3. *She phones you/She'll phone you* if she can't come.

4. *What did you do/What will you do* if you miss your plane?

5. *If I get home this evening/When I get home this evening,* I'll phone my mother.

6. *When he leaves school,/Whenever he leaves school,* he wants to go to university.

7. *I give her a kiss,/I am giving her a kiss* whenever I see her.

8. I'm going by train if *I will get a ticket./I can get a ticket.*

9. When I am the last to leave, *I always shut the back door./I'll shut the back door.*

10. I will be quite surprised if *he passes the exam./he will pass the exam.*

11. I go on holiday in December if *I have enough money./I'll have enough money.*

12. If you find money on the street, *may you give it to the police?/will you give it to the police?*

13. *If Janet is at home this evening,/If Janet will be at home this evening,* I'll visit her.

14. If I am late, *I take a taxi./I'm taking a taxi.*

15. Whenever the wind blows from the south, *it gets cold./it got cold.*

EXERCISES
Zero and First conditionals.

Unscramble these sentences using the correct alternative.

Look at the example.

weekend If this rains, I home stay it stay at **I'll**.
*If it rains this weekend, **I'll** stay at home.*

Now you try.

1. I may have the if visit going holiday long Andes I a want.

2. degree Sarah university David has unless won't he marry if a.

3. I buy to the popcorn cinema, I some go buy Whenever I'll.

4. me When, go I to my work, I with whenever take lunch.

5. If unhappy he most marries he, will her married be.

6. shoplifting from steal a have, it's shop you stolen called If.

7. stop must red was when You the traffic light is.

8. A petrol is if it car runs stops out stopping of.

9. If it's you you taste known sea know water, you'll salty.

10. if happy winning He isn't he's unless.

11. If boyfriend tells wait to my comes, him tell.

12. catch we leave bus, we'll now Unless the miss bus will.

13. was excuse late Whenever has he is clever, he a.

14. planning They to to a bigger a move plan if he house gets raise.

15. What lottery hoping are do you if will you the win?

EXERCISES
Second and Third conditionals.

Put in the correct verb form.

Look at the example.

If it rained this weekend, I_____at home.
If it rained this weekend, I'd stay at home.

Now you try.

1. If I had nothing to do, I_____to the library.
2. My ex-wife would invite me to dinner whenever I_____her.
3. What_____you   if you hit a cat with your car?
4. He wouldn't tell you unless you_____him.
5. If you found money on the street,_____you_____it to the police?
6. He'd have married the girl of his parents' choice if they_____him to.
7. Unless they bought tickets to the game, they_____in.
8. The plants wouldn't grow if they_____any water.
9. You_____what they were talking about unless you_____the book.
10. She_____the Louvre if she got the chance to visit Paris.
11. I_____to work if my office was nearer.
12. Unless he_____more, he wouldn't win the match.
13. If there_____a fire in this building, what would you have done?
14. If I were late, I_____a taxi.
15. you_____away if you saw a snake?

EXERCISES
Second and Third conditionals.

Choose the correct alternative. In some instances two alternatives might be right.

Look at the example.

If it rained this weekend, I'll *stay at home./'d have stayed at home./'d stay at home. If it rained this weekend,* **I'd stay at home**.

Now you try.

1. If he left school, he*'d have worked as a printer./'d work as a printer./ works as a printer.*

2. She*'ll phone/'d phone/has phoned* if she couldn't come.

3. I'd have been quite surprised if she*'ll pass/passed/had passed* the exam.

4. If I were travelling by train, I *book/'d book/'d have booked* early.

5. I'd visit Japan if I *can speak/could speak/could've spoken* Japanese.

6. If you changed your mind, *would/will/can* you tell me?

7. I*'d have been/'d be/will be* very sick if I had drunk so much alcohol.

8. If she came to the party, she*'d meet/'ll meet/met* some interesting people.

9. Had I set my alarm, I*'d have woken up/'d have woke up/wake up* in time.

10. I*'d buy/'d have bought/will buy* that car had I wanted to.

11. If you had't been absent from class, you*'ll know/know/'d have known* about the test.

12. If he listened to the instructor, he*'d make/made/'ll have made* fewer mistakes.

13. Had she asked for my opinion, I *won't/wouldn't have/won't have* given it to her.

14. If I *knew/had known/can know* she would slap my face, I wouldn't have kissed her.

15. He*'d feel/feels/'ll felt* a lot better if he went to the doctor.   .

EXERCISES
Second and Third conditionals.

Unscramble these sentences using the correct alternative. There are some words you don't need. Look at the example.
~~stayed~~ home it at this, If ~~have~~ I ~~I'll~~ rained'd stay weekend.
*If it rained this weekend, **I'd stay** at home.*

Now you try.

1. took I had a brought camera, I'd sunset taken picture a If have of the.

2. film saw have it seen enjoyed will if would you had You the.

3. She lift have you a give if given her been car would hadn't gave stolen.

4. would have had lend you lent He money if the he it.

5. If you she visited were was in would knew hospital, you have had her.

6. could will earlier have if come they, had They caught the can train.

7. She something angry get would may if said I will.

8. done bought Had I computer a buy better, I have do could more.

9. If listened happening to known the they listening news, what would know they was.

10. had wouldn't humans have didn't a thumb, would be a lot there they do couldn't If.

11. I couldn't to went Spain, watch If I wouldn't the watched bull-fighting.

12. I saw been have would If in they trouble, seen had be me.

13. If been were away cage the flew open, the would bird fly.

14. it was very been broken, I had would breaks have If angry.

15. If had the she questions right asked has, would she some gets have interesting got answers.

EXERCISES
CONJUNCTIONS
Put an appropriate conjunction in the gap.

Look at the example.

I'll go to the movies_____I have time.
*I'll go to the movies **if** I have time.*

Now you try.

1.   We will go to the party_____we don't have to go to the hospital.

2.   We are thinking of renting a car_____we have to go to Hamilton in a hurry.

3.   They didn't buy the house_____cit was beautiful.

4.   She won't marry him_____he buys her a house.

5.   He can't speak English_____he has been here for 10 years.

6.   They bought a lot of money with them_____they wanted to buy a house.

7.   They won't go_____they have been invited.

8.   _____his good looks, she refused to marry him.

9.   He continued playing_____his broken arm.

10. I won't buy a car_____the bus service is excellent.

11. I won't win at tennis_____I practise every day.

12. I'll take it_____he offers it to me.

13. Fast food has a lot of fat, it_____has a lot of sugar.

14. _____he is very rich, she won't marry him.

15. He was eating too often_____he became overweight.

EXERCISES
Put the appropriate conjunction in the right place in the sentence.

Look at the example.

I'll go to the movies I have time.
*I'll go to the movies **if** I have time.*

Now you try.

1. She married that man he was poor.

2. You may go to the party you have finished your homework.

3. We made it to the train on time the bus arrived late.

4. the teacher the student here.

5. The bakery had to close early it had run out of bread.

6. He was playing out in the rain he caught a cold.

7. He has been very unhappy his wife left him.

8. I enjoyed the movie my headache.

9. He caught the early bus he had to be home for dinner.

10. I'd known you were coming, I'd have baked a cake.

11. He decided to stay in school later he had some homework to finish.

12. Every one worked fast they could go home early.

13. the teacher the students here.

14. he was running down the stairs, he slipped and broke his leg.

15. John and Albert are twins. Mary and Shirley are twins.

EXERCISES
Unscramble these sentences and put in the appropriate conjunction.

Look at the example.

have l go the to time movies I'll.
*I'll go to the movies **if** I have time.*

Now you try.

1. You you're lost look.

2. my my holiday sister on parents away are.

3. the class the teacher in was students.

4. 30th, you by the the you can pay join classes.

5. They storm back on Hamilton driving insisted to the.

6. not chocolate hungry I resist cannot I'm

7. married the she her years, was fact older twenty he.

8. never promises again the he to talk me him to buy world! I'll

9. She game pretty a tennis of squash her good awful! is plays.

10. borrow You can bring my midnight you it back car by.

11. they was this to would it restaurant so to going knew be expensive, never They have come.

12. train to leave down the I The was station running the began stairs.

13. Sarah a expensive bought a very house car.

14. overnight toothbrush I'm take have to my going I to stay.

15. I'll tickets have any to I'll now not leave get.

EXERCISES
GERUNDS

Put the gerund form of the verb provided in the gap.

Look at the example.

I like_____. *(eat)*
*I like **eating**.*

Now you try.

1. _____is a very cheap exercise. *(walk)*

2. Some people are always trying to avoid_____tax. *(pay)*

3. They are not interested in_____for a new house. *(look)*

4. After all the_____, she is looking forward to_____in her own bed. *(sleep/travel)*

5. They are thinking of_____on their house to their children. *(pass)*

6. She is wondering about_____him nor not. *(marry)*

7. I am used to_____with the radio on. *(study)*

8. Some games start with the_____of a coin. *(flip)*

9. The bad weather prevented us from_____on time. *(leave)*

10. Martha apologized for_____my birthday. *(forget)*

11. I quit_____twenty-five years ago. *(smoke)*

12. Have you considered_____your job? *(change)*

13. Andrew thought_____the bus was a good idea. *(catch)*

14. They put off_____a party because their child fell ill. *(give)*

15. Susan spends most of her free time_____. *(shop)*

EXERCISES
Put the gerund form of the verb in brackets in the right place in the sentence.

Look at the example.

I like. *(eating)*
*I like **eating**.*

Now you try.

1. When I finish tonight I'm going to see a movie. *(study)*
2. I'll keep here till I find a better job. *(work)*
3. Jenny spent all day for the dinner party. *(prepare)*
4. He was lying in bed a book when he heard a strange noise. *(read)*
5. the price of the product was not a good idea. *(raise)*
6. I saw a man under the street light. *(stand)*
7. What are you considering with your old car? *(do)*
8. Mathew discussed the army with his parents. *(join)*
9. The boss suggested work early today. *(stop)*
10. When I saw the cat slip on a banana peel, I couldn't stop. *(laugh)*
11. We mustn't avoid our dues. *(pay)*
12. I don't mind people in their own language in front of me. *(speak)*
13. Some Catholics give up meat for lent. *(eat)*
14. They delayed the house till they sold their own. *(buy)*
15. I appreciate your me a lift to the airport. *(give))*

EXERCISES
Unscramble these sentences.

Look at the example.

eating like I.
*I like **eating**.*

Now you try.

1. buying are of house They thinking that.

2. another looking you for considered a Have job?

3. Buddhist Nina became gave when meat up she eating a.

4. apologized for Tony teacher being to late his.

5. eating meals I to used am not big.

6. English to improve movies is good a the way to your Going.

7. good had a They leaving not soon reason for so.

8. She her is finding in interested out about ancestry.

9. button can off pushing by turn the machine You this.

10. closing I know responsible who is the don't for office.

11. shoes aren't walking used They to without.

12. I'm good giving is sure him money a not idea.

13. music you listening like to classical Do?

14. said river from Nothing we stopped swimming him the.

15. look I the your forward attending to wedding.

EXERCISES
INDIRECT SPEECH

Rewrite the sentences in their reported form using the appropriate reporting verb.

Look at the example.

Peter said, 'I like you Mary.'
*Peter **told** Mary **he liked her**.*
*Peter said **(that) he liked** Mary.*

Now you try.

1. Janet always says, 'I'm too busy.'

2. My daughter asked, 'Can I show you my homework?'

3. He asked me, 'Where are you from?'

4. Our boss said, 'You can all go home early today.'

5. She replied, 'Yes. I'll marry you.'

6. The boy said, 'May I give my homework later?'

7. The shop assistant announced, 'The shop is closing in ten minutes.'

8. His father said, 'Can't you shut up for a minute?'

9. The team manager said, 'We aren't playing this weekend.'

10. Mary asked Jane, 'Have you seen the film?'

11. He told his girlfriend, 'I have a surprise for you.'

12. I was asked, 'What do you do for a living?'

13. My boss asked us, 'Could you all come in early tomorrow?'

14. The police officer said, 'Leave the premises.'

15. Peter said, 'I wouldn't have seen that film if you hadn't suggested it.'

EXERCISES
INVERSION

Rewrite these sentences in their inversion form.

Look at the example.

Push the button **to start the engine**.
To start the engine, *push the button.*

Now you try.

1.   She put a flower behind her ear.
2.   The light went out with a pop.
3.   The smoking gun lay on the bed.
4.   I apologize for being rude to you yesterday.
5.   There was a lot of rubbish at the door of the house.
6.   We stopped at a petrol station after driving through the night.
7.   People were waiting for more than four hours at the airport.
8.   They have been living here since they came to New Zealand.
9.   I can't buy that car with the money I have.
10. He put a rose into his button hole.
11. The boys jumped on the train at the last minute.
12. He turned the corner driving as fast as he could.
13. The diamond ring was found under the carpet.
14. The winning goal was scored at the last minute.
15. He crept in through the window.

EXERCISES
MODALS

Put the appropriate modal in the gap provided.

Look at the example.
I_____sing but I_____play the piano.
*I **can** sing but I **can't** play the piano.*
*I **can't** sing but I **can** play the piano.*

Now you try.

1. You_____come late to class.

2. What_____you like for your birthday?

3. He_____spend less if he wants to save money.

4. When I was a child, I_____n't eat cabbage.

5. _____you open this bottle for me, please?

6. I don't think Peter_____like this movie.

7. I_____touch that snake, if I were you.

8. _____you like to come with us?

9. I'm sorry, you_____n't come to my party last week.

10. Where_____I find a good shoe shop?

11. I_____if you_____.

12. Do you think you_____write a book one day?

13. _____I come in?

14. In New Zealand we _____drive on the left.

15. He's not studying much, but he_____pass.

EXERCISES
Put the appropriate modal in the right place in the sentence.

Look at the example.

I sing but I play the piano.
*I **can** sing but I **can't** play the piano.*
*I **can't** sing but I **can** play the piano.*

Now you try.

1. You smoke in restaurants.
2. You be impolite to others.
3. you dry the dishes?
4. I'm sorry. I lend you my car this weekend.
5. You drink and drive.
6. That is a very good film, you see it.
7. I forget to buy a present for my mother.
8. We leave early today; the traffic is going to be very bad.
9. I'm tired already; I have gone to bed earlier.
10. Peter has promised; he take the children to the zoo.
11. I love to go to the cinema with you.
12. you pass the sugar?
13. He have caught the bus if he had left sooner.
14. I go to bed late tonight; I have to catch an early plane.
15. The lesson was quite difficult; the teacher explain it very well.

EXERCISES
Unscramble these sentences and then put in the right modal in the right place.

Look at the example.

sing I I piano play the but.
*I **can** sing but I **can't** play the piano.*
*I **can't** sing but I **can** play the piano.*

Now you try.

1. tomorrow I up to early; I plane have wake a catch.
2. cake like this to try you?
3. marry you Mary cousin her Do think?
4. dancer the good is prize, he Harry a win very.
5. invitation accept George's Helen?
6. I think today it rain don't.
7. were I eat you meals between if I.
8. right be This.
9. Take rain an, umbrella it.
10. the begin movie When?
11. I These. too salty eat are them chips.
12. the coming, the You window shut rain's in.
13. You a look see very doctor well, don't you.
14. languages Matthew four speak.
15. now like to you order?

EXERCISES
SEMI-MODALS

Put the appropriate semi-modal in the gap provided. There could be several possibilities, try as many as you can.

Look at the example.

I_____go home now.
I ought to/want to/have to/would like to/need to/am going to go home now.

Now you try.

1. I_____start university next year after I finish my English course.
2. Do I_____do the homework by tomorrow?
3. My friends_____have my birthday party at a restaurant.
4. I'd rather have gone to the cinema tonight, but I_____study for my exam.
5. You don't look well, you_____see a doctor.
6. They_____get married in the spring.
7. We_____buy a house in a few years time.
8. You don't_____come if you don't_____.
9. He_____get to the airport on time.
10. You_____be here by 11.00 pm.
11. Every year many brave men and women_____climb Mt. Everest.
12. Albert and Cynthia_____come to the show; it's too expensive.
13. Do you_____play tennis with me?
14. You don't_____give me a present for my birthday.
15. When they were children, they_____live on a farm.

EXERCISES

Put the appropriate semi-modal in the right place in the sentence. There could be several possibilities, try as many as you can.

Look at the example.

I go home now.
I ought to/want to/have to/would like to/need to/am going to go home now.

Now you try.

1. In my country, I coach a boxing team.
2. you buy some cheap books?
3. I think I go to bed now.
4. Who do the cooking for tomorrow night?
5. you visit the Louvre?
6. I start exercising, I'm getting too fat!
7. I wouldn't put my hand into a lion's mouth.
8. They read the article before they came to class.
9. Prue get a better job soon.
10. Now the children feed themselves.
11. Jack pay his bill by last Thursday.
12. Where you stay when you get to Shanghai?
13. The children read before they go to sleep.
14. They speak English a few months ago.
15. She make the cake for the party, but she forgot.

EXERCISES
Unscramble these sentences and then put in a semi-modal in the right place. There are several possibilities, try as many as you can.

Look at the example.

home now go I.
*I **ought to/want to/have to/would like to/need to/am going to** go home now.*

Now you try.

1. don't don't you that You buy house if.
2. come to child's if dinner doesn't well She, her not.
3. What meeting say did the they at?
4. station you to How get the?
5. computer buy new We a.
6. month He by finish degree his next.
7. meet parents you my?
8. world She always around has sail the.
9. football boots You have won't unless play you the right.
10. Atlantic a of people Ocean lot the row Not across.
11. to get the on We taxi time find concert because we a.
12. tonight go Do to concert you a?
13. me I bed a child When, was I doll take my to with.
14. meeting the come to Harold tonight.
15. couldn't your Sorry go, I come hospital to party, I to the.

EXERCISES
NEGATIVES

Put a negative form in the gap. Look at the example.

I_____a teacher.

*I **am not** a teacher.*
*I'**m not** a teacher.*

Now you try.

1. She_____like cooking.

2. They_____going to go to the cinema tonight.

3. You_____drink and drive.

4. Muslims_____allowed to drink alcohol.

5. Prue_____sing very well but she can dance beautifully.

6. Harry_____got the courage to ask her.

7. I_____go out in this weather if I were you.

8. He_____like his father at all.

9. I_____go to his party even if he invites me personally.

10. That painting_____done by Picasso.

11. In New Zealand you_____drive on the right.

12. John and Martha_____married but they live together.

13. You have seen that film,_____you?

14. He_____like ice cream at all.

15. The well_____full of water when I looked into it.

EXERCISES
Put a negative form in the right place in the sentence. Some sentences need two negatives.

Look at the example.

I a teacher.
*I **am not** a teacher.*
*I'**m not** a teacher.*

Now you try.

1.   We planned our holiday yet.

2.   They been living here long.

3.   The boys go out; they finished their homework.

4.   K2 as high as Mount Everest.

5.   He plays football very well, he?

6.   The police think he was the murderer.

7.   You lie to me, would you?

8.   The book returned to the library in time so he had to pay a fine.

9.   The children phoned their parents yet.

10. Why you come to my party?

11. I am a teacher, I?

12. If I were you, I go down that street.

13. You be late or you'll miss the bus.

14. She ever seen her father.

15. She been given the keys to the house so she go in.

EXERCISES
Unscramble these sentences and put in the correct negative form. Some sentences need two negative forms.

Look at the example.

teacher a I.
*I **am not** a teacher.*
*I'**m not** a teacher.*

Now you try.

1. book I last interesting read week The.
2. Albert his anyone shoes. Has find them seen?
3. water There's in swim the. pool We.
4. one's here smoke to in allowed.
5. forgiven ever ex-boyfriend her She.
6. likes cream everyone eating ice.
7. I go the unless to movies tickets with pay for you you the.
8. you Are us sure come want you to with?
9. climb We hill that, we could?
10. ages lived She here for.
11. have You to if want come you to.
12. would happen You to $5.00, have you?
13. exercise you this do?
14. Brian come may.
15. he I exam when failed surprised the.

EXERCISES
NOUNS

Put in the correct form of the words provided in brackets.

Look at the example.
The_____has two new_____. *(tooth/baby)*
The **baby** has two new **teeth**.

Now you try.

1. The_____lives in the Indian_____. *(tiger/jungle)*

2. No one can have complete_____in their lives. *(happy)*

3. She found a nest of_____under the floor. *(mouse)*

4. I found these_____in a very old_____. *(bookshop/book)*

5. He couldn't remember the_____of the_____who wrote
    the_____. *(novel/name/author)*

6. Would you like to go_____next weekend? *(swim)*

7. They went to the dairy and bought some_____, an_____and
    a_____. *(drink/chips/ice cream)*

8. I mind people_____in restaurants. *(smoke)*

9. To do crosswords you need some_____.*(intelligent)*

10. She met_____at her sister's_____two years ago. *(wedding/
    Jonathan)*

11. During our_____, we climbed three_____. *(mountain/holiday)*

12. I was thinking of_____that_____but I changed my_____*(mind/
    buy/house)*

13. Could you please stop_____so much! *(talk)*

14. in the park is very good_____. *(exercise/walk)*

15. is the capital of_____. *(New Zealand/Wellington)*

EXERCISES
Unscrambles these sentences and put in an appropriate noun. Some sentences might need two or more words.

Look at the example.

is improve good your way a to.
Reading is a good way to improve your **vocabulary**.
Listening is a good way to improve your **pronunciation**.
Walking is a good way to improve your **fitness**.

Now you try.

1. the somewhere here is His near.
2. marrying is.
3. Andrew himself buying enjoy doesn't for.
4. to skills radio a the listening good develop is way to your.
5. Zealand in Do enjoy you New?
6. sport a people dangerous is think Some.
7. has The next beautiful a door.
8. get old you to have be do to a How driver's?
9. the The left they rang house just as.
10. was bottle half-full The of.
11. TV Turn the the and on watch.
12. The clouds through shone the.
13. can find Do where you know I a good?
14. of garden full Her was sweet-smelling.
15. A house in my cost friend's a painting lot of.

EXERCISES
PREFIXES

**Complete the prefix in each sentence with the appropriate verb or noun.
Look at the example.**
Robert Hawkins is an **a**_____, he doesn't believe in god.
*Robert Hawkins is an **atheist**, he doesn't believe in god.*

Now you try.

1. Smoking marijuana is still **il**_____in some countries.

2. For humans to fly like birds is **im**_____for the moment.

3. The children are happy to spend weekends with her **ex-**_____.

4. It looks like more and more people are becoming **anti-**_____.

5. IBM is **a multi-**_____organization.

6. Research is showing that more people than ever are **over-**_____.

7. Most European countries had to be **re**_____after World War 2.

8. Almost every house now has a **micro**_____.

9. As soon as we got to the hotel, we **un**_____our bags.

10. Quite a few language teachers are **bi**_____.

11. I'm sorry, I don't think you're right; I must **dis**_____with you.

12. Actors used to use **pseudo**_____instead of their real names.

13. Usain Bolt has **out** _____everyone in the 100 metre race.

14. My **co-**_____are very pleasant to work with.

15. UNICEF is a **non-**_____organization.

EXERCISES
Choose the correct word in the brackets to complete the sentences.

Look at the example.

Robert Hawkins is an; he doesn't believe in God *(theist/atheist)*
*Robert Hawkins is an **atheist**; he doesn't believe in God.*

Now you try.

1. Harriet is a, she speaks several languages. *(monolinguist/ multilinguist)*

2. Our teacher asked us all to move in an direction. *(anticlockwise/ anteclockwise)*

3. The United States has the most in the world. *(submarines/ semimarines)*

4. I'm sorry, I you for someone I knew. *(misled/mistook)*

5. This copier is very old; it is always. *(malfunctioning/maltreating)*

6. She is most her brother. *(dislike/unlike)*

7. People who commit mass murders are. *(incorrect/insane)*

8. The other day, I had a very experience. *(non-expected/unexpected)*

9. It wasn't expensive because it was only a stone. *(semi-precious/ semi-circular)*

10. We all attended a parade. *(pro-dawn/pre-dawn)*

11. I do all my shopping at my local. *(supersete/supermarket)*

12. We had to return our steaks to the kitchen, they were. *(subcooked/ undercooked)*

13. Being rude to customers is. *(counter-intuitive/counter-productive)*

14. People who don't believe in right and wrong are. *(amoral/atheist)*

15. He is a student of Philosophy. *(subgraduate/postgraduate)*

EXERCISES
The prefixes provided at the end of the sentences are incorrect. Unscramble the sentences and put in the correct form of the prefix in the correct place. The underlined words are proper nouns.

Look at the example.

God <u>Robert Hawkins</u> an; believe he doesn't is in *(atheism)*
<u>*Robert Hawkins*</u> *is an **atheist***; he doesn't believe in God.

Now you try.

1. train the because timetable missed train <u>James</u> and the. *(unread)*

2. by years her <u>Margaret</u> husband 10. *(pastlived)*

3. towns most Anzac Day On parades are there in. *(post-dawn)*

4. don't that teams are than more successful Teams that. *(reoperate)*

5. very be people When are they tired can. *(nonpatient)*

6. child's <u>Ms Jones</u> the my school is of. *(semi-principal)*

7. them photos good are; we These very should. *(inlarge)*

8. a is country <u>Saudi Arabia</u>. *(bitheist)*

9. very amusing is <u>Noel's</u>. *(semibiography)*

10. dangerous be can chicken very. *(malcooked)*

11. In metro <u>Paris</u> the it's, in it's <u>London</u> the in the and <u>New York</u> it's. *(underway/subground)*

12. practice In times, the to common ancient it enemy was. *(inslave)*

13. fat The getting main for reason is. *(outeating)*

14. at are There speed can planes travel that. *(panasonic)*

15. very The a is <u>durian</u> fruit. *(miniodorous)*

EXERCISES
Put in the appropriate prefix that matches the sentence.

The first two have been done for you.

	statement	what prefix fits
1	I am against war!	anti-war
2	This letter is not right, I'm going to write it again.	rewrite

Now you try.

3	This answer is not correct.	
4	She speaks two languages.	
5	I visit my doctor twice a year.	
6	I need to empty my suitcase.	
7	That man is so rude!	
8	I can't see it, it's behind the building.	
9	I don't think you are right!	
10	There are a lot of people who have no work.	
11	It's easy to ride this, even though it has only two wheels.	
12	He's not a very friendly person.	
13	I need to take this medicine for my cold.	
14	I liked the teacher from my last class.	
15	He is always in a hurry.	
16	I buy this magazine two times a month.	
17	My homework was not good so I did it again.	
18	The pilot put the plane on automatic.	
19	He is not like his father.	
20	She doesn't like horror movies.	
21	He doesn't believe babies should be killed before birth.	
22	I just met my boss from my last job.	
23	We had to stop the machine because it got too hot.	
24	He thinks this government is pretty good.	
25	I agreed with the Cuban revolution.	
26	Smaller and smaller computers are being made.	
27	Tiny, tiny things; germs for example.	
28	Some of this translation is not correct in English.	
29	Sorry, I thought you said I should come today.	
30	The Nazis hated the Jews.	
31	I am studying for my Master's degree.	
32	After the revolution everyone was happy.	
33	This machine is very good for reheating food.	
34	I will never agree to go to war.	
35	I disagree with the government all the time.	
36	It's 4 o'clock and the bank is closed. I was told banks close at 5 pm.	
37	The only reason people get fat is that they eat too much.	
38	IBM is an international company.	
39	A computer can be used for many things.	
40	Sorry, I'm late. My alarm didn't ring.	

EXERCISES
SUFFIXES

Complete each sentence with the appropriate suffix. Remember to change the spelling where necessary.

Look at the example.

Robert Hawkins isn't a *the*_____; he doesn't believe in god.
*Robert Hawkins isn't a **the<u>ist</u>**, he doesn't believe in god.*

Now you try.

1. Even though Peter's in his twenties, he sometimes behaves in a very
    child _____way.

2. They had a very happy **child**_____.

3. The **interview**_____was upset by the questions and left
    the interview.

4. The police did not believe his **deny**_____of the robbery.

5. The economic **develop**_____of China has been very rapid.

6. In New Zealand, the police don't have the **author**_____to
    carry weapons.

7. She looked at her mother with very **sleep**_____eyes.

8. Mary is a very kind person; she isn't **self**_____at all.

9. Some magazines **glamour**_____the lives of celebrities.

10. The **block**_____in the pipe was cleared by the engineer.

11. The U.S.A doesn't like the idea of **commune**_____.

12. They walked **happy**_____down the road.

13. Kangaroos cannot move **back**_____.

14. Smoking is a very **harm**_____habit.

EXERCISES
Choose the correct word in brackets to complete the sentences.

Look at the example.

Robert Hawkins isn't a *(theist/atheist)*; he doesn't believe in God
*Robert Hawkins isn't a **theist***; he doesn't believe in God.

Now you try.

1. *(Foolishness/Friendship)* is very important in people's lives.

2. She has a very *(catty/catlike)* walk.

3. A *(scientist/chemist)* works in a pharmacy.

4. The *(Brazilians/Brazilese)* are good at football.

5. Greece is considered the first *(democracy/democratic)* country.

6. We were all deeply *(saddened/sadly)* by the news of her death.

7. *(Chemistry/Chemical)* warfare is illegal.

8. The River Nile is the *(longer/longest)* river in the world.

9. Playing sport is very *(healthful/healthy)*.

10. His *(generosity/generousness)* impressed everyone.

11. Hemingway's novels are quite *(readable/readible)*.

12. He has a *(youngly/youngish)* look about him.

13. The *(inhabitants/inhabitees)* of Mongolia are still nomadic.

14. The swimming pool has been *(lengthy/lengthened)*.

15. The sunset was quite *(magicive/magical)*.

EXERCISES
Unscramble the sentences and choose the correct word provided at the end of the sentence.

Look at the example.

God Robert Hawkins a; believe he doesn't isn't in *(theism/theist)*
*Robert Hawkins isn't a **theist**;* he doesn't believe in God.

Now you try.

1. me movie That. *(boring/bored)*

2. her was She for selected. *(beauty/beautiful)*

3. a in We nice live very. *(neighbourhood/neighbourly)*

4. The fine told that him he doctor was. *(healthy/health-wise)*

5. office the went post They. *(forward/towards)*

6. of Most countries have form Middle-East a. *(democracy/democratic)*

7. ships on work. *(Sailists/Sailors)*

8. country a New Zealand very is. *(pictureful/picturesque)*

9. multi-national is Telecom a. *(organization /organizational)*

10. is Queen Street. *(noisy/nosey)*

11. office allowed the Are the smoke to in? *(employees/employed)*

12. moment not The is in the at; 4.00 pm will here be she at. *(doctoress/ doctor)*

13. red the does What colour? *(signify/signified)*

14. an is woman She. *(attracted/attractive)*

15. spoke He. *(quiet-like/quietly)*

EXERCISES
PREPOSITIONS

Complete the sentences with the appropriate preposition.

Look at the example.

The train left_____8.30 am.
*The train left **at** 8.30 am.*

Now you try.

1. Can we all meet___the restaurant?

2. Have you been waiting here_____8.00 am?

3. I have been learning English_____three years.

4. I'm not upset_____people speaking_____their own language.

5. He's an actor, but__the day he works_____a teacher.

6. Airplanes usually leave___time.

7. We were___time for the train; in fact, we had time for a coffee.

8. It was good to hear the students speaking to each other____English.

9. I sat_____the café_the bus arrived.

10. John is____for the moment, would you like to leave a message?

11. Do you know who the owner_____this car is?

12. I have quite a few red shirts_____my clothes.

13. We visited the Smiths, but they weren't____.

14. Albert never goes anywhere_____his wife.

15. She met her husband_____her holidays.

EXERCISES
Put the appropriate preposition in the correct place. Some sentences may need more than one.

Look at the example.

The train left 8.30 am.
*The train left **at** 8.30 am.*

Now you try.

1. Yesterday was the hottest day yet; it was 40°.
2. We haven't heard them they left New Zealand.
3. The boy kicked the ball the window and broke it.
4. Could you put the picture the clock the wall?
5. There were some interesting trailers the movie began.
6. Is the school the bus stop?
7. He always talks if he is a policeman.
8. I will only wait here 3.00 pm.
9. The train doesn't go Wellington. Wellington you need take a bus.
10. The cinema is the post office; that's why you can't see it here.
11. Harriet woke up early go a run.
12. It's good see you're time once.
13. There were two major wars the last century.
14. The cost houses goes every year.
15. They ran when they saw the police.

EXERCISES
Unscramble the sentences and put in the appropriate preposition in the correct place.

Look at the example.

8.30 train The am left.
*The train left **at** 8.30 am.*

Now you try.

1. things is A cutting knife.
2. dancer very is A a mine friend good.
3. this houses old street very are The.
4. visa do I get What do have a?
5. was house trees The the.
6. is doctor he What a?
7. the The was cat sleeping car.
8. his uses hairbrush a He shoebrush.
9. Paris often bridges sleep the Vagrants.
10. is the What hill name that?
11. question asked When him I the, hurry went he a.
12. his goes He wife holiday always.
13. Why mystery she me him a married is.
14. asked story me go police my The again.
15. movie the we went restaurant a.

EXERCISES
Put in the correct preposition in the space provided. There is one blank.

The alarm clock rang_____6.50 am. I reached out a warm arm
from_____the duvet and turned the radio_____. The news
was_____Fiji. I looked_____the window, the sky was covered clouds,
some birds flew_____the trees_____the garden and I could hear
a dog barking_____the distance.

I got_____of bed and slipped my feet_____my slippers and
put_____my dressing gown. I then went_____the kitchen and opened
the fridge. I took_____a bottle_____milk_____the fridge and
called_____the cat. She came running_____me when she heard my
voice. I poured some milk_____her bowl and put the milk_____in
the fridge.

I, then, went_____the bathroom_____have a shower. I noticed
there were no clean towels so I had_____get one_____the cupboard
which was_____the hand basin. I took_____a large red one,
which I put_____the towel rail. I have a special habit_____how
I arrange my toilet. I put my razor_____my shaving cream and
my toothbrush_____the toothpaste and my aftershave cream. I
usually brush my teeth_____I have my shave, but this morning I
decided_____have my shave_____I brushed my teeth.

While I was brushing my teeth I turned_____the shower_____let
the warm water start. When the warm water started I finished brushing my
teeth and got_____the shower. After my shower I put my shaving things
and my toothbrush and left the bathroom. I put the wet towel_____the
window so it would dry_____the hot sun.

breakfast, I sat_____in front_____my computer and prepared
this lesson_____my class. I hope they can choose_____the right
preposition_____the wrong one. If they can, it means they have understood
the lesson, which will be good. I am meeting them_____university
9.00 am; we will meet_____class. I hope this will be good
practice_____learning prepositions.

EXERCISES
PRONOUNS

Put an appropriate pronoun in the space provided. Look at the example.
The book is on the table._____put_____there.
*I/You/He/She/They/We put **it** there.*

Now you try.

1. Peter caught the train on time._____caught_____at 3.30 pm.

2. The boys make their own beds._____make_____.

3. Mary put her coat in the wardrobe._____put_in the wardrobe.

4. The boy makes his own breakfast. ____makes _____breakfast_____.

5. Ask May to put the book there. Ask_____to put_____there.

6. Where is the pen that belongs to me? Where is_____pen?

7. My brother and I liked playing together._____liked playing together.

8. John borrowed Peter's car._____borrowed_____car.

9. Jane and Mary bought the house together._____bought____together.

10. John's bed was made by my mother and I.___bed was made by____.

11. This is my book. This book is_____.

12. These birds don't fly._____don't fly.

13. My book isn't as good as your book._____isn't as good as_____.

14. Cats clean their own bodies._____clean_____.

15. Look at those birds fighting! Look at_____fighting.

EXERCISES
Put in the appropriate pronouns.

Look at the example.

Peter took dog for a walk but ran away
*Peter took **his** dog for a walk but **it** ran away.*

Now you try.

1. Mary returned books to the library; had finished reading.

2. and sister went on a holiday together; was a lot of fun.

3. Where did put the cheese? can't find anywhere.

4. children loved the present gave them; gives a lot of pleasure.

5. can't give to; doesn't belong to.

6. Albert, is a maths teacher, also coaches boxing.

7. The boys were playing by when mother got home.

8. Who gave these shirts? look awful!

9. This is the woman car bought.

10. neighbours have decided to give a party.

11. Is this the dress would like to buy?

12. Peter is the person from bought golf clubs.

13. Young as is; can dress.

14. Did you see? was very exciting, wasn't?

15. can't decide if wants to marry or not!

EXERCISES

Each sentence has two or more pronouns; unscramble the sentences and use the correct pronoun(s).

Look at the example.

them bus went the cinema to *They* by.
They went to the cinema by bus. **Them** is extra.

Now you try.

1. Jane hers Mary book gave her to.

2. It's black is Its colour.

3. mine book you Have got my?

4. Is my yours this mine you or?

5. themselves painted They house Them his ourselves their.

6. I herself took himself He cinema off to the.

7. hair is She hers playing always with him.

8. book your It's yours.

9. hers pass it you me its Can to?

10. yours book is you Which?

11. you hisself he house this make doll's yourself Did?

12. young They can't She he herself go to shops the by ourselves, she too is.

13. I to my mine, forgot yoursYou borrow can bring I you?

14. They happy We very; are they we like new their ours house.

15. himself is to always He talking hisself.

EXERCISES
PUNCTUATION

Put the appropriate punctuation in the correct place.

Look at the example.

next year Im thinking of visiting china mongolia korea and japan
<u>N</u>ext year I'm thinking of visiting <u>C</u>hina, <u>M</u>ongolia, <u>K</u>orea and <u>J</u>apan.

Now you try.

1. if the weather is fine Ill go for a walk

2. he lives in paris hes lived there for five years

3. im thinking of buying a new car do you think its a good idea

4. the usa is in north america

5. I dont want to go alone cant you come with me

6. what a horrible man she said

7. all the girls shoes are on the verandah

8. the old man and the sea was written by earnest hemingway

9. these babies parents are from romania

10. ive lost my book its cover is blue

11. she is a happy cheerful confident baby

12. is this your pen do you think i can borrow it

13. my sister who is a teacher lives in toronto

14. Ive seen blazing saddles many time its a very funny movie

15. some of the things we need to buy are cheese bread butter cauliflower etc

EXERCISES
Rewrite these passages and put in the necessary punctuation in the right place.

Look at the example.

next year Im thinking of visiting china mongolia korea and japan
Next year I'm thinking of visiting China, Mongolia, Korea and Japan.

Now you try.

1. well the book didnt interest me at all till i heard a talk on the radio titled books and then i took notice and bought the book it was an interesting read

2. do you spend a lot of time travelling

3. theres a hotel in ispahan iran called caravanserai the floor in the foyer is made of a translucent material through which a soft light shines in the middle there is a water fountain in the traditional iranian style the water sprays upwards in the green white and red colours of the national flag at least thats how i remember it

4. yesterday mary her sister and two friends went to the shopping mall where they bought several items of clothing a skirt some lipstick and a pair of stockings then they went to the hoyts cinema and watched a film called pirates of the caribbean they enjoyed it very much and thought johnny depp was really very funny

5. where did they come from one minute there was no one here the next the place is full of people fat thin arabs indians europeans and they all seem to know each other who are they

EXERCISES
APOSTROPHE

Change these sentences using an apostrophe.

Look at the example.

Those girls always sit at that table.
That is those girls' table.

Now you try.

1. The shirt which belongs to this boy is red.

2. I have not got any pens.

3. I am not going to see the movie *Blue Blood*. It is rubbish.

4. The boots of those boys are in the corner.

5. They have gone to Spain and will not be back till July.

6. I would have bought the house if they had dropped the price.

7. The teachers books are in this room.

8. The Jones house burned down last night.

9. I could not have passed the exam even if I had studied harder.

10. I will go to the party only if Mary does not come.

11. I could not buy the car; I did not have enough money.

12. You must not come late to class.

13. They are happy playing in the house of Peter.

14. If they had been invited, they would have come.

15. They will not leave until they have been paid.

EXERCISES
CLOSED QUESTIONS

Put the correct auxiliary verb /modal in these closed questions. There are several choices.

Look at the example.

_____you going away this weekend?

Are *you going away this weekend?*

Now you try.

1. _____we playing tennis this weekend?
2. _____you be here tomorrow afternoon?
3. _____they enjoy living in Indonesia?
4. _____she been married long?
5. _____Monday a holiday?
6. _____you keep this chair for me?
7. _____she finished the letter?
8. _____they at the party last night?
9. _____the children break the window?
10. _____you think it will rain tomorrow?
11. _____they like to buy this car?
12. _____it raining when you left the house?
13. _____he phoned his mother yet?
14. _____she planning to change her job?
15. _____they leave when they have finished?

EXERCISES
Unscramble these questions into their correct form.

Look at the example.

weekend you Are away the for going?
Are you going away for the weekend?

Now you try.

1. away you weekend Did go last?

2. truck drive Can Tom a?

3. yet his Has he got licence?

4. make Did this you cake?

5. an you for Could half wait hour?

6. they Were yesterday late?

7. you horse ever Have off a fallen?

8. he accident Was in injured the?

9. he old twenty-five Is over years?

10. go to walk you for Would a like?

11. play Can come the out to children?

12. Peter on Did leave time?

13. next give Do to a party want they Saturday?

14. today the I office leave May early?

15. Anne here tomorrow Will be?

EXERCISES
Unscramble these questions. The auxiliary verbs /modal and main verbs are missing. There may be more than one way to complete the questions.

Look at the example.

year you this to on holiday?
*Are you **planning** to **go** on holiday this year?*
*Are you **going** to **go** on holiday this year?*
*Will you **go** on holiday this year?* (and so on)

Now you try.

1. to you my Friday next party?
2. to tennis like table you?
3. snake ever you a?
4. waiter the I?
5. to you I next?
6. butter please me the, you?
7. word you meaning this the of?
8. the *Don Quixote* you book?
9. music listening you classical to?
10. if me I house had you big a?
11. I you?
12. to tomorrow it rain?
13. doctor to you be a.
14. opera she?
15. have the salary right job if you the was?

EXERCISES
OPEN QUESTIONS

Divide the sentence into its pieces of information (parts of speech), then ask questions about each piece of information.

Look at the example.

Peter works in a factory.

1 subject	2 verb	3 object (place)
Peter	*works*	*in a factory.*

QUESTION				ANSWER
Who			*works*	*in a factory?*	**PETER**
What	*does*	*Peter*	*do?* *		**WORKS ...**
Where	*does*	*Peter*	*work?*		**in a FACTORY**

Remember the rule for asking questions about verbs **(p154)**. **Now you try:**

1.   Peter worked in a factory last year.

QUESTION					ANSWER
Who					**PETER**
What			*		**WORKED ...**
Where					**in a FACTORY**
When					**LAST YEAR**

2.   Peter works with John in a factory

QUESTION					ANSWER
Who					**PETER**
What	does		*			**WORKS ...**
Who(m)	does		**			**JOHN**
Where	does			**		**in a FACTORY**

** **with** is required.*

3. Peter is working with John in a factory today.

QUESTION					ANSWER
who					PETER
What			*	**	WORKING ...
Who(m)		**			JOHN
Where				**	a FACTORY
When				**	TODAY

4. Hamilton is about a 100 kms from Auckland.

QUESTION					ANSWER
	city				HAMILTON
	far				about 100 kms
	city				AUCKLAND

5. Peter can swim very well.

QUESTION					ANSWER
					PETER
			*		SWIM
	well				VERY well

6. Peter took his sister to school yesterday.

QUESTION						ANSWER
						PETER
			*			TOOK ...
						HIS SISTER
						SCHOOL
						YESTERDAY

7. Peter has bought a house.

QUESTION				ANSWER
				PETER
			*	BOUGHT ...
				A HOUSE

EXERCISES
Put in the missing question word and the accompanying auxiliary verb /modal.

Look at the example.

_____John go yesterday?
Where did John go yesterday?
Now you try.

1. _____you last week?
2. _____Peter buy you for your birthday?
3. _____she going to the party with?
4. _____you been?
5. _____movies_____you seen this month?
6. _____I show my passport to?
7. _____you doing your homework?
8. _____that person talking to you sister?
9. _____book_____you reading now?
10. _____all the flowers gone?
11. _____I buy some really good clothes?
12. _____the movie going to begin?
13. _____book_____lying under the table?
14. _____the best film you've seen this year?
15. _____happy_____you to see your family?

EXERCISES
Unscramble these questions.

Look at the example.

going marry Who Mary is to?
Who is Mary going to marry?

Now you try.

1. restaurant recommend Chinese would Which you?

2. buy bananas How $5.00 can many I for?

3. going is away how Jonathan to long be For?

4. with person lovely Who that the is smile?

5. going car we Whose are in?

6. name is What animal of the that?

7. doggie window in How that the much is?

8. should for a I do What headache?

9. lost students their have Which books?

10. car colour your What was?

11. whom give To ticket you did the?

12. at you are What looking?

13. you How eaten biscuits many have?

14. a dollars What won do you if you would million?

15. next are you Where your to going go holidays for?

EXERCISES
Unscramble these questions. There are two words missing in each question.

Look at the example.

you you What phoned doing I?
What --- you doing --- I phoned you?
*What **were** you doing **when** I phoned you?*

Now you try.

1.   here before studying Where you you?

2.   is movie the seen you What ever?

3.   petrol price of these the days?

4.   moon from is How the?

5.   for we $5.00 What?

6.   bus you What on?

7.   nice like on to a, sunny you do day?

8.   you did house for pay your?

9.   house you Which in?

10. you money you your lost feel all How?

11. take your How petrol car?

12. window the?

13. next the Wellington is train?

14. Auckland have How you in?

15. car To his Andrew old sell?

EXERCISES
TAG QUESTIONS

Complete these statements with the correct tag question.

Look at the example.

Mary is a good dancer,
*Mary is a good dancer, **isn't she**?*

Now you try.

1. You are from Ireland,_____?
2. They played a very good game of football,_____?
3. She won't come to your party,_____?
4. The Smiths have left for Spain,_____?
5. Nobody was interested in going to the zoo,_____?
6. We mustn't be noisy,_____?
7. He bought his pen in that shop,_____?
8. They haven't seen that film yet,_____?
9. One shouldn't be rude to others,_____?
10. Kiwi birds can't fly, _____?
11. The boys want to play on their computers,_____?
12. He broke his leg playing hockey,_____?
13. She does look beautiful,_____?
14. You would love to play the piano well,_____?
15. I am good at tennis,_____?

EXERCISES
QUESTIONS WITH HOW

Unscramble these questions. There is an extra word in each question.

Look at the example.

bag How serious is heavy your?
How heavy/~~serious~~ is your bag?
*How **heavy** is your bag?*

Now you try.

1. can fly heavy How far a bird?

2. How watch boring expensive your was?

3. have much How friends do many you?

4. How fat Sky Tower the tall is?

5. How hours you long do each English your practise many day?

6. interesting boxing you How interested are in?

7. interested was saw How movie night exciting the you last?

8. much drink How tea many do you?

9. much week do money many spend you each How?

10. rotate Earth How does usually often the?

11. often usually in How rain it New might Zealand?

12. phone many much have you your times lost How?

13. restaurant have How many you in often eaten that?

14. go fast long a sports can How car?

15. Street How fast is long Queen?

EXERCISES
RELATIVE PRONOUNS & CLAUSES

Put in the correct relative pronoun in each sentence.

Look at the example.

This is the man_____lives down the street.
*This is the man **who** lives down the street.*

Now you try.

1. Mary once lived in a house_____was 400 years old.

2. She is the woman_____looked after me when I was ill.

3. Mary,_____he sold his house, is a lawyer.

4. Do you know anybody_____repairs Persian carpets?

5. This is the time_____Peter goes for a run.

6. Jennifer loves reading books_____are romantic.

7. Can you tell me_____car that is?

8. This is the place_____he parks his bike.

9. The policeman_____I was stopped by, was very polite.

10. The man_____is walking his dog is a detective.

11. She is the actor_____won two Oscar awards.

12. The man_____a visa was issued turned out to be a con-man.

13. The country_____I want to visit most is Spain.

14. I'd like to meet the architect_____work this is.

15. Can you suggest_____wine I should order?

EXERCISES
Connect the sentences with the pronoun in brackets. Some changes might be necessary.

Look at the example.

This is <u>a</u> man. He lives down the street. *(who)*
*This is <u>the</u> man **who** lives down the street.*

Now you try.

1. Last year they visited a country. The country was very beautiful. *(which)*

2. I remember a day. I got married that day. *(when)*

3. She was very nice. I met a woman at a party. *(whom)*

4. They were walking in a park. The trees were very green. *(where)*

5. We could see a man. He was standing on his head. *(who)*

6. He fixed the problem. We don't know what he did. *(how)*

7. He has gone back to India. His family is there. *(where)*

8. He is doing something. I don't know anything about it. *(what)*

9. I looked at a painting at the art gallery. It was beautifully done. *(that)*

10. This is a car. Its owner is Bill. *(whose)*

11. He came to New Zealand. He settled happily. *(where)*

12. This is his friend. He brought him a souvenir from Cuba. *(whom)*

13. Saturday is the day. We do our grocery shopping then. *(when)*

14. In our school there were children. Some didn't have shoes. *(who)*

15. I spoke to a man. He gave me directions to the hospital. *(who)*

EXERCISES
Connect these sentences using a relative pronoun. Some changes might be necessary.

Look at the example.

This is <u>a</u> man. He lives down the street.
*This is <u>the</u> man **who** lives down the street.*

Now you try.

1. He is an accountant. He does my accounts.

2. They are workmen. They repaired our roof.

3. He is a racing car driver. He won the Grand Prix last year.

4. She is my best friend. I bought her an expensive present.

5. She is an artist. She gave me a beautiful painting.

6. This is a book. It has some very beautiful pictures.

7. He is my neighbour. His car is a Lamborghini.

8. This is the time. All good men must stand up and be counted.

9. This is the reason. He can't attend the meeting.

10. A woman came into the room. She was wearing a purple dress.

11. This is the room. I left my book here.

12. Do you know the man. Emma is talking to him.

13. This is a man. I borrowed his book.

14. They are singers. They were hired by the company for three weeks.

15. I ate in a restaurant last night. It had delicious food..

EXERCISES
Unscramble these sentences and replace the pronoun with the relative pronoun. Some sentences might not require a relative pronoun.

Look at the example.

road is the down This lives man he the.
*This is the man **who** lives down the street.*

Now you try.

1.   countryside year was they it a Last house in bought the.
2.   I a book it written reading am Saki was by.
3.   the shoes them liked the he I was party wearing at.
4.   car going into fast A was mine crashed it very.
5.   seller by best is The written a Harold it book was a.
6.   for loan book asked it was she the out The on.
7.   200 I letter it ago was a found written years.
8.   book I left it a on belonged the library bus to the.
9.   the gave He man the him was to $5000,00 government.
10.   party girl He a met a she him invited to.
11.   playing woman well-known badminton Albert with is a. She is.
12.   trees neighbour house round lot in a it lives has a of My.
13.   can't the gave yesterday problem do them They you it to.
14.   The shorts wearing was tennis playing man he red was.
15.   him gave a the Maori book it 14th century was She about life in.

EXERCISES
Complete the sentence with the appropriate pronoun and relative clause from the box.

Look at the example.

| ~~he is an engineer.~~ | ~~that came late to work.~~ | sings very well.√ |

This is the man_____.
This is the man **who sings very well**.

Now you try.

| were made in France. /party they went to. /she has a lot of money. /painting is in the window. /the boss came in. /called *The Rocky Horror Show*. /had once been his wife. /has that interesting story? /their grandmother gave them. /was about dogs. /stole the famous painting? /you want to buy? / the sun shines every day. /I catch the bus. /made her parents very happy. /previous owner was a careful driver. /from where she can see the sunset. /is far from the city. |

1. This is the girl

2. Those are the cars

3. Is he the man?

4. The elderly lady always sits

5. I'm looking forward to going on holiday

6. She would like to live in a beach house

7. They are going to see the movie

8. Margaret won a prize for her short story

9. We bought a car

10. 8.00 am is

11. The children are playing a computer game

12. They enjoyed the company of the woman

13. Is this the book?

14. He was looking at a photograph of the woman

15. Where did you put the book

EXERCISES
Shorten or truncate the sentences.

Look at the example.

The man [who is (wearing) the red shirt] is a famous footballer.
*The man **wearing the red shirt** is a famous footballer.*
*The man **in** the red shirt is a famous footballer.*

Now you try.

1. The men who were standing under the lamplight were plainclothes policemen.

2. The boy who is bouncing the ball is a good footballer.

3. The women playing netball in the black and white uniforms are world champions.

4. The dagger which was stolen from the museum is worth hundreds of dollars.

5. The people who are walking down the street have just graduated from university.

6. The book that is on the table has some beautiful pictures.

7. The suitcase that was left on the bus belonged to my uncle.

8. Can you pass me the magazine that is lying on the sofa?

9. The car which is parked in front of my house is a stolen car.

10. The doctors who are wearing the blue gowns are surgeons.

11. The house which was built 200 years ago sold for 2 million dollars.

12. The cattle that are walking through the gate belong to my neighbour.

13. *The Great Gatsby*, which was written by F. Scott Fitzgerald, is very popular.

14. The note which was pinned to my door has disappeared.

15. We are going to visit the castle which is in Malta.

EXERCISES
TENSES

Present simple & Present continuous.

Put the correct form of the verb in brackets in the sentence. Some sentences are in the passive form

Look at the example.

John_____to school on his bicycle every day. *(go)*
*John **goes** to school on his bicycle.*

Now you try.

1. Marjorie_____to her friend on her mobile phone at the moment. *(talk)*

2. The students_____homework every day. *(give)*

3. Peter_____in being loyal to his friends. *(believe)*

4. Nowadays most cars   air conditioning. *(have)*

5. The police_____blue uniforms. *(wear)*

6. Their parents_____away on a business trip today.*(go)*

7. _____that boy_____near here? *(live)*

8. The weather_____very quickly on islands. *(change)*

9. Albert_____to jazz. *(listen)*

10. Her flat_____located on the third floor. *(be-verb)*

11. Where_____Cynthia_____her clothes? *(buy)*

12. Water_____to steam when it is boiled. *(turn)*

13. The boys who_____football_____to that school. *(play/belong)*

14. The animals_____fed by the zoo keepers. *(be)*

15. She_____her parents every evening. *(email)*

EXERCISES
Present simple & Present continuous.

Complete the sentence with the correct form of the verb in the correct place. Some sentences are in the passive form.

Look at the example.

John to school on his bicycle.
*John **goes/is going** to school on his bicycle.*

Now you try.

1. Muslims don't pork.

2. These students one book a week.

3. These clothes made in China.

4. Where they?

5. My sister and her family in Canada at the moment.

6. Taxis usually driven by immigrants.

7. the police?

8. The girls who the blue uniforms very good at netball.

9. The music they to very popular.

10. The desert very little rain.

11. Beer drunk all over the world, except in Muslim countries.

12. Some evenings I dinner.

13. My dog doesn't a tail.

14. What time they?

15. Please the window, it's cool in here.

EXERCISES
Present simple & Present continuous.

Unscramble these sentences choosing the correct verb. Some sentences are in the passive form.

Look at the example.

to on bicycle John school goes his ~~going~~. *(**going** is wrong because there is no be-verb) John **goes** to school on his bicycle.*

Now you try.

1. sun is The warm shining the and day shine is.

2. is schools teaching not in most taught Religion.

3. They very live in a lives house old.

4. looks lovely look She. bright always is wearing She very colours wears.

5. How you Hamilton go do to are? are there driving We drive.

6. think about are you What thinking?

7. playing am likes liking I tennis.

8. most TV enjoyed programme children is This enjoying by.

9. Those flies are birds trees into flying the.

10. waiting at are people outside The the wait moment cinema the.

11. flowing The Sea into Nile River the Mediterranean flows.

12. sleeping class He always is sleep in.

13. beautifully is woman dresses That dressing.

14. The put is books putting on shelves librarian by the the.

15. this you Are book Do buying?

EXERCISES
Past simple & Present perfect.

Put in the correct form of the verb in brackets. Some sentences are in the passive form.

Look at the example.

John_____to school on his bicycle yesterday. *(come)*
*John **came** to school on his bicycle yesterday.*

Now you try.

1. I_____that film several times. *(see)*

2. Where_____you_____? I_____you for a long time. *(see/be)*

3. Apollo 11_____on the moon on the 20th of July, 1969. *(land)*

4. Marlon Brando was_____his first Oscar in 1955. *(award)*

5. _____you_____to Margaret yet? *(spoken)*

6. He's a boxer; his nose_____several times. *(break)*

7. The children_____their visit to the zoo three weeks ago. *(enjoy)*

8. They still_____from their son in Australia. *(hear)*

9. When_____Apollo 11_____on the moon? *(land)*

10. Who_____*The Old man and the Sea*_____by? *(write)*

11. I_____already_____lunch. I_____at Dino's. *(have/eat)*

12. Angela_____her house two months after she_____in New Zealand. *(buy/arrive)*

13. Christina_____on a farm when she_____a child. *(be/live)*

14. There_____two burglaries on our street last night. *(be)*

15. _____the students_____to yet? *(speak)*

EXERCISES
Past simple & Present perfect.

Complete the sentence with the correct form of the verb in the correct place. Some sentences are in the passive form.

Look at the example.

John to school on his bicycle yesterday.
*John **came** to school on his bicycle yesterday.*

Now you try.

1. It all day yesterday.

2. The house after the owner.

3. Lucy her driving licence several months ago.

4. Paul his old car.

5. Who these photos? They are beautiful.

6. you the movie you last night?

7. My watch made in Switzerland.

8. These students here for six months.

9. There ten people in the room when the manager in.

10. They want to leave so I the police.

11. The play last night for two hours.

12. Do you know when they the top of Mt Everest?

13. How you your hand? It looks painful.

14. We our best clothes to the wedding.

15. No, thank you. I just some.

EXERCISES
Past simple & Present perfect.

Unscramble these sentences choosing the correct form of the verb. Some sentences are in the passive form.

Look at the example.

to on bicycle John school went his yesterday ~~going~~. (**going** is wrong because there is no be- verb)
*John **went** to school on his bicycle yesterday.*

Now you try.

1. was often actor famous for mistaken She mistook a.
2. his The hid sister hide boy little from.
3. wind swept has ocean sweeped across the The.
4. I stung was bee by stinging a.
5. laid on child She the lies bed gently the.
6. for These were breeding dogs bred racing.
7. quit the She quitting after company her an with argument boss.
8. The 4.00 setting has alarm be for set been am.
9. through childhood pilot dreaming his he All dreamed becoming was of a.
10. The destroyed destroying was house fire by.
11. us The shook all hands with king shaken of.
12. all forecast for has was yesterday been wrong The.
13. wear She has what going chosed she is chosen to.
14. The bed go children have all to gone.
15. told leave to telling were We room the.

EXERCISES
Past simple & Past continuous.

Put in the correct form of the verbs provided in brackets

I (wait)_____in the doctor's surgery for my appointment when a man (enter)_____the room. He (wear)_____a balaclava and carrying a hammer in his left hand. I (think)_____to myself, 'Don't panic!' Easier said than done. To show how calm I (be)_____, I (pick)_____up a newspaper and (pretend) to read. While I pretend)_____to read I (keep) looking over the top of the paper at the man who (be) now (sit)_____by the door, staring directly in front of him. It so (happen) _____that I was (place) directly in the line of his gaze. It is in moments like these that one wants to resort to some comedy: two eye holes bored through the centre of the paper so that I could observe him without being (observe)_____myself for instance. Just as I (think)_____of how I (will) manage to make the holes, the doctor (enter)_____and (summon) me to his room. What a relief! The doctor_____(not) mention the man in the waiting room, so neither did I. The doctor (look)_____into my ear when I (hear)_____a creepy sound – 'What (be)_____that fellow up to?'

EXERCISES
Past simple, Past continuous & Past perfect.

Complete the sentence with the correct form of the verb(s) in the correct place. Some sentences are in the passive form.

Look at the example.

John to his school on his bicycle yesterday.
*John **went** to school on his bicycle yesterday.*

Now you try.

1.   She the movie so she before it.
2.   Steve the money but he want to give it to me.
3.   The girls to the mall when they their parents.
4.   The flag at dawn.
5.   A man into me and my ice cream to the ground.
6.   He just his memoirs when he.
7.   you finally buy the house? Yes, I it.
8.   The balloons up by the children.
9.   Who the hat with the feather on it?
10. The dictionary back on the shelf.
11. The sheep by a wolf.
12. The elderly lady her lips sipping on the hot coffee,
13. They at a lot of houses before they the right one.
14. She money from the ATM machine when she.
15. The train into the station while we in the cafe.

EXERCISES
Past simple, Past continuous & Past perfect /continuous.

Unscramble these sentences choosing the correct form of the verb. Some sentences are in the passive form.

Look at the example.

To hitted school on was he John his go hit when a going bicycle tree.
*John **was going** to school on his bicycle when he **hit** a tree.*

Now you try.

1. party Julia at was the had? she was What wear wearing?
2. talking was The busily to students other were when walks lecturer each in walked the.
3. house built we tents; lived was lives While our being in.
4. I library the university yesterday have visited; were a of quietly lot students are studying.
5. We stroll strolling park through us the; a ran were up our dog dropped to is and running a at feet ball.
6. raining because They it decided rained to a taxi were home take was.
7. We struck were up when the striking packs the earthquake packing tent.
8. legs the was being ran carried up bed stairs the; the While cat run between carrying our.
9. Herbie was been classes hadn't so haven't attending he disqualified.
10. The stolen statues taking being to were the are taken museum were when they.
11. window I sit bird sitting by into crashing the a While crashed was it.
12. football Simon watching on is TV had while his yard playing watches children been were in the.
13. ave was at her She worked giving sneak when fright working I snuck computer up and a her.
14. were the was children shown being What been?
15. had The car been was accident of the from scene removed moving the.

EXERCISES
TWO Ts OR NOT TWO Ts

Here are a few words to practise on.
Remember: *Long vowel sounds; don't repeat the last letter (L). Short vowel sounds; repeat the last letter (S). And remember the* **consonant/vowel/ consonant** *rule!*

base verb	continuous	past continuous	3rd/past perfect
beat (L)	beating	beat	beaten
begin (S)	beginning	began	begun
bite (L)	biting	bit (S)	bitten

Now you try.

cut			
eat			
forget			
get			
hit			
hurt			
lend			
mean			
meet			
put			
read			
ring			
run			
set			
shut			
swim			
wear			
win			
write (L & S)			

Do a few of your own here.

EXERCISES
PARTS OF SPEECH

Name the parts of speech and write a sentence of your own similar (almost) to the example.

Look at the example.

The	boys	are swimming	in	the	river.
*definite article (dart)**	*plural common noun (plctcn)*	*present continuous (prc)*	*preposition (pr)*	*definite article (dart)*	*common noun (sgctcn)*

You can use the symbols on **page 18, if you wish.*

The	*children*	*are playing*	*on*	*the*	*swing.*

Now you try.

1

You	are	very	hot
and	would	like	to
open	the	window.	

Write your own sentence here.

2

I	am	a	student,
I	come	from	Russia.

Write your sentence here.

3

You	can't	see	the
board	because	the	teacher
is	standing	in	front
of	it.		

Write your own sentence here.

4

The	boy	woke	up
and	went	to	the
window.			

Write your own sentence here.

5

My	room-mate,	Leo,	is	20.

Write your sentence here.

6

I	sometimes	go	to
the	movies	on	Saturdays,

Write your sentence here.

7

What	do	you	do
in	the	evenings?	

Write your sentence here.

8

John	and	Mary	live	in
a	very	big	house.	

Write your sentence here.

9

They	were	listening	to
the	news	when	the
police	arrived.		

Write your sentence here.

10

While	she	was	lying
on	the	grass,	a
dog	ran	over	her.

Write your sentence here.

AND FINALLY . . .

Teaching or learning a language is a game: it requires play and a lot of practice, so play and practice.

Feel free to challenge the contents of this book—all contrary opinions and suggestions (and praise) are welcome, just email me <u>at ferooz@clear.net.nz.</u>

The attempt is to make English grammar—for teaching ESL—more accessible than most other grammar books I have encountered. If this has not been the case; let me know. There is more going on in my head than I put down in this book.

In the meantime, enjoy the book and continue to enjoy teaching English as a second language. It's a bloodless sport.

Kia ora

ferooz

ANSWER KEY

This section contains answers to only the more complex exercises. Most of the gapfill exercises should be easy for the learner to complete. The exercises are titled by their Parts of speech (Adjectives) or their structure (Conditionals) followed by the page number; hence the first exercise is **Adjectives 183**

Adjectives 183

1. Mary isn't as **tall/friendly** etc., as her brother.

2. Do you know which is *the** **tallest/newest**, etc., building in the world?

3. The Chinese/Koreans are very **different** *from**/**similar** *to** the Koreans/Chinese.

4. I feel **hungry**; I think I'll have an apple.

5. I have a shirt *the* **same** colour as yours.

6. Her baby is **taller** *than**/**heavier** *than, etc.,* mine.

7. She and I know he is a **friendly/clever** etc., person.

8. Dogs are **friendlier**/*more* **friendly**/*more* **popular**, etc., *than* cats.

9. The dress she is wearing is **similar** *to* mine.

10. I'm planning to buy a very **expensive** pair of shoes.

11. Paul Getty used to be *the* **richest** man in the world.

12. She looked **lovely/wonderful** in that **wonderful/lovely** dress.

13. This test was **easier** *than/more* **difficult** *than* the last one.

14. It was *the most** **expensive**/*the* **fastest** etc., meal I had ever eaten.

15. Jennifer is *the most* **popular**/*the most* **interesting** etc., student in the school.

16. *the italicized words are necessary to these adjectives.*

Adjectives 188

1. The Bentley is an **expensive** car.

2. Sky Tower is **higher** *than* the ASB building

3. Could you suggest an **exciting** novel?

4. He gave us a very **interesting** explanation.

5. Hemingway wrote several **dramatic** novels.

6. The blue whale is **larger *than*** an elephant.

7. I bought a **cheap**, **Indian**, **cotton** shirt. *(See pg. 68 for Adjective order)*

8. Some people thing Steinbeck is a **better** writer ***than*** Hemingway.

9. Who is that man **standing** by the door?

10. The police are looking for the **stolen** painting.

11. Some people think the Mona Lisa is ***the* greatest** picture ever painted.

12. Tokyo is ***more* populated *than*** Hong Kong.

13. Are you **sure** she can't come to the party?

14. John look so **depressed**; he must have failed his exam.

15. That was a very **generous** offer; I had to accept it.

Adverbs 191 These are only sample answers.

1. The students' English is getting better

    because they are speaking more.
    getting **much** better.

2. The Smiths haven't left the country

    since they arrived.
    for many years.

3. Where will you be

    in ten years time?
    when they arrive?

4. **When he was a young man,**

    Before he became a football coach,
    he was a teacher.

5. Is there **anywhere/somewhere** you would like to go?

6. I'm really happy. I've **just** bought a house.

7. Have you **ever** touched a snake?

8. She is having her party on

> **the 3rd of December.**
> **the last Saturday in December.**

9. **Just as we were about to leave,**

   At sunset,

> the sky began to cloud over.

10. I couldn't sing very well before

> **I took singing lessons.**
> **the age of 10.**

11. Since **coming to New Zealand,**

> **taking private lessons,**
> my English has improved.

12. When they heard the noise, they left

> **in a hurry.**
> **by the back door.**

13. Henry's birthday is on

> **the 6th of June.**
> **Wednesday.**

14. I can't see you **tomorrow,**

> **this weekend,**
> I have to go to Hamilton.

15. My neighbours have been living here

> **since 2001.**
> **for a very long time.**

Of course, there are many more ways to completing these sentences.

Adverbs 192

1. Do you **always/usually** have your coffee here?

2. The Sahara Desert can get **very/extremely** hot.

3. Electronic technology has made **quite/very** rapid progress.

4. People are **always/frequently** leaving things behind on the bus.

5. No, thank you. I've **just/already** had some.

6. I started collecting stamps **when I was at school** etc.

7. We don't **usually** have classes on Tuesdays.

8. How **often** do you visit your parents?

9. **How many** books has Jack written?

10. I don't **often/usually** drink coffee.

11. Have you bought the car **yet**?

12. Are they **still** living in the same house?

13. The weather got **so** hot; I had to stop for a rest.

14. I **never** etc., go to the movies.

15. It's difficult to hear her; she talks too **softly**.

Articles 195

1. Could you come in early to **the** office tomorrow morning?

2. Don't hang **the** painting/clock under **the** clock/painting.

3. Harvard is one of **the** best universities in **the** world.

4. I waited for her for **an** hour at **the** hotel, but she didn't come so I went to **the** cinema.

5. **The** buying and selling of illegal drugs is **a** universal problem.

6. Everest is **the** highest mountain in **the** world.

7. Is it okay for **the** boys to go out and play in **the** park?

8. When I was **a** university student, I drove around in **an** MR2.

9. **The** Missouri River is **the** longest river in **the** United States.

10. Can you pass **the** butter, please?

11. She didn't learn to play **the** piano when she was **a** child at school.

12. Most of **the** world was at war in **the** 1940s.

13. I don't think I can pass **the** test; I haven't put in enough work.

14. They drove around **the** European countryside looking for **an/a** hotel;

15. **The** highest mountain in **the** North Island is Mount Ruapehu./Mount Ruapehu is **the** highest mountain in **the** North Island.

Auxiliary verbs 199

1. I **have** just had breakfast.

2. They **are** doing their homework.

3. She **was/is** wearing a red dress.

4. **Have** you ever touched a snake?

5. Harold **was** living in London when he met his wife.

6. **Did/Does** he take the train to Paris?

7. Sally **has** never been to China.

8. **Is** he sitting by the window?

9. Somebody **has** stolen my bike.

10. **Are** they thinking of buying a car?

11. **Are** you looking for a good restaurant?

12. The sun **was** shining when I left the house.

13. He **was** driving too fast when he hit the tree.

14. What **do** you do in the evenings?

15. What **does** she do for a living?

Conditionals 202

1. I may visit the Andes if I have a long holiday.

2. Sarah won't marry David unless he has a university degree.

3. Whenever I go to the cinema, I buy some popcorn.

4. When I go to work I take my lunch with me.

5. If he marries her, he will be most unhappy.

6. If you steal from a shop, it's called shoplifting.

7. You must stop when the traffic light is red.

8. A car stops if it runs out of petrol.

9. If you taste sea water, you'll know it's salty.

10. He isn't happy unless he's winning.

11. If my boyfriend comes, tell him to wait.

12. Unless we leave now, we'll miss the bus.

13. Whenever he is late, he has a clever excuse.

14. They plan to move to a bigger house if he gets a raise.

15. What will you do if you win the lottery?

Conditionals 205

1. If I had brought a camera, I'd have taken a picture of the sunset.

2. You would have enjoyed the film if you had seen it.

3. She would have given you a lift if her car hadn't been stolen.

4. He would have lent you the money if he had it. /He would lend you the money if he had it.

5. If you knew she was in hospital, you would have visited her.

6. They could have caught the train if they had come earlier./If they had come earlier, they could have caught the train.

7. She would get angry if I said something.

8. Had I bought a better computer, I could have done more.

9. If they listened to the news, they would know what was happening.

10. If humans didn't have a thumb, there would be a lot they couldn't do.

11. If I went to Spain, I wouldn't watch the bull-fighting.

12. If they had seen me, I would have been in trouble.

13. If the cage were open, the bird would fly away.

14. If it had broken, I would have been very angry.

15. If she had asked the right questions, she would have got some interesting answers.

Conjunctions 207

1. She married that man **even though/although** he was poor.
2. You may go to the party **if/when** you have finished your homework.
3. We made it to the train on time **even though** the bus arrived late.
4. **Both** the teacher **and** the student **are** here.
5. The bakery had to close early **because** it had run out of bread.
6. He was playing out in the rain **so** he caught a cold.
7. He has been very unhappy (ever) **since** his wife left him.
8. I enjoyed the movie **in spite of** my headache.
9. He caught the early bus **because** he had to be home for dinner.
10. **If** I'd known you were coming, I'd've baked a cake.
11. He decided to stay in school later, **because/as** he had some homework to finish.
12. Everyone worked fast **so** they could go home early.
13. **Both** the teacher **and** the students **are** here.
14. **While** he was running down the stairs, he slipped and broke his leg.
15. John and Albert are twins, Shirley and Mary are **also** twins (**also**).

Conjunctions 208

1. You look **as if** you're lost.
2. **Both** my parents **and** my sister are away on holiday.
3. **Neither** the students **nor** the teacher **was** in class./**Neither** the teacher **nor** the students **were** in class.
4. **Provided/ Providing/If** you pay by the 30th, you can join the class.
5. They insisted on driving back to Hamilton **in spite of** the storm.
6. I cannot resist chocolate **even if** I'm not hungry.
7. **Despite/In spite of** the fact she was twenty years older, he married her.
8. I'll never talk to him again, **even if** he promises me the world.
9. She plays a pretty good game of tennis/squash, **however,/but** her squash/tennis is awful.

10. You can borrow my car **if** you bring it back by midnight.

11. They would never have come to this restaurant **if** they knew it was going to be so expensive.

12. The train began to leave the station **as** I was running down the stairs.

13. Sarah bought a house **and** a very expensive car.

14. I'm going to take my toothbrush **in case** I have to stay overnight.

15. I'll have to leave now **or** I'll not get any tickets.

Gerunds 210

1. When I finish **studying** tonight, I'm going to see a movie.

2. I'll keep **working** here, till I find a better job.

3. Jenny spent all day **preparing** for the dinner party.

4. He was lying in bed **reading** a book when he heard a strange noise.

5. **Raising** the price of the product was not a good idea.

6. I saw a man **standing** under the street light.

7. What are you considering **doing** with your old car?

8. Mathew discussed **joining** the army with his parents.

9. The boss suggested **stopping** work early today.

10. When I saw the cat slip on a banana peel, I couldn't stop **laughing**.

11. We mustn't avoid **paying** our dues.

12. I don't mind people **speaking** in their own language in front of me.

13. Some Catholics give up **eating** meat for lent.

14. They delayed **buying** a house till they sold their own.

15. I appreciate your **giving** me a lift to the airport.

Gerunds 211

1. They are thinking of buying that house.

2. Have you considered looking for another job?

3. Nina gave up eating meat when she became a Buddhist.

4. Tony apologized to the teacher for his being late.

5. I am not used to eating big meals.

6. Going to the movies is a good way to improve your English.

7. They had a good reason for not leaving so soon.

8. She is interested in finding out about her ancestry.

9. You can turn off the machine by pushing this button.

10. I don't know who is responsible for closing the office.

11. They aren't used to walking without shoes.

12. I'm not sure giving him money is a good idea.

13. Do you like listening to classical music?

14. Nothing we said stopped him from swimming the river.

15. I look forward to your attending the wedding.

Indirect speech 212

1. Janet always says (that) she is too busy.

2. My daughter asked (me) if she could show me her homework.

3. He asked me where I was from.

4. Our boss said (that) we could all go home early_____.*

5. She replied she would marry_____**./She agreed to marry_____**.

6. The boy asked if he might give his homework later.

7. The shop assistant announced (that) the shop was closing in ten minutes time.

8. His father asked if_____** couldn't shut up for a minute./His father told_____** to shut up.

9. The team manger told/informed us (that) we weren't playing that* weekend.

10. Mary asked Jane if she had seen that film.

11. He told his girlfriend (that) he had a surprise for her.

12. I was asked what I did for a living.

13. My boss asked us if we could *** all come in early the next day*.

14. The police officer told/ordered_____** to leave the premises.

15. Peter said (that) he wouldn't*** have seen that film if I**hadn't*** suggested it.

* **time**: choose the relevant time.
** **person**: choose the relevant person being spoken to.
*** **'past' modals** don't change.

Inversion 213

1. Behind her ear,* she put a flower.
2. With a pop the light went out./Out with a pop went the light.
3. On the bed lay the smoking gun. On the bed the smoking gun lay.
4. For being rude to you yesterday, I apologize.
5. At the door of the house (there) was a lot of rubbish.
6. After driving through the night we stopped at a petrol station.
7. For more than four hours people were waiting at the airport.
8. Since they came to New Zealand they have been living here.
9. With the money I have I can't buy that car.
10. Into his button hole he put a rose.
11. At the last minute the boys jumped on the train.
12. Driving as fast as he could he turned the corner.
13. Under the carpet the diamond ring was found.
14. At the last minute the winning goal was scored.
15. (In)** through the window he crept (in).

*commas are optional
** more dramatic but either position is OK.

Modals 215

1. You **mustn't** smoke in restaurants.
2. You **shouldn't/mustn't** be impolite to others.
3. **Could/Can** you dry the dishes?
4. I'm sorry. I **can't** lend you my car this weekend.
5. You **mustn't** drink and drive.

6. That is a very good film, you **should/must** see it.

7. I **mustn't** forget to buy a present for my mother.

8. We **should/must** leave early today; the traffic is going to be very bad.

9. I'm tired already; I **should** have gone to bed earlier.

10. Peter has promised; he **must** take the children to the zoo.

11. I **would** love to go to the cinema with you.

12. **Could/Can** you pass the sugar?

13. He **would/could** have caught the bus, if he had left sooner.

14. I **shouldn't/mustn't** go to bed late tonight; I have to catch an early plane.

15. The lesson was quite difficult; the teacher **couldn't** explain it very well.

Modals 216

1. I **must** wake up early tomorrow; I have a plane to catch.

2. **Would** you like to try this cake?

3. Do you think Mary **will** marry her cousin?

4. Harry is a very good dance, he **should/will** win the prize.

5. **Will/Should** Mary accept George's invitation?

6. I don't think it **will** rain today.

7. I **wouldn't** eat between meals if I were you.

8. This **should/could/may**, etc., be right.

9. Take an umbrella, it **may/could** rain.

10. When **will** the movie begin?

11. These chips are too salty. I **can't** eat them.

12. You **should** shut the window, the rain's coming in.

13. You **should** see a doctor, you don't look very well./You don't look very well, you **should** see a doctor.

14. Matthew **can** speak four languages.

15. **Would** you like to order now?

Semi-modals 218

1. In my country, I **used to** coach a boxing team.

2. **Would** you **like to** buy some cheap books?

3. I think I **have to*** go to bed now.

4. Who **wants to*** do the cooking for tomorrow night?

5. **Would** you **like to** visit the Louvre?

6. I **have to** start exercising, I'm getting too fat!

7. I wouldn't **dare to** put my hand into a lion's mouth.

8. They **had to** read the article before they came to class.

9. Prue **is hoping to*** get a better job soon.

10. Now the children **are learning to** feed themselves.

11. Jack **had to** pay his bill by last thurssday.

12. Where **are** you **going to** stay when you get to Shanghai?

13. The children **like to** read before they go to bed.

14. They **learned to** speak English a few months ago.

15. She **was supposed to*** make the cake for the party, but she forgot.
*There could be several possibilities.

Semi-modals 219

1. You don't **have to** buy that house if you don't **want to**.

2. She doesn't **have to** come to dinner if her child's not well.

3. What did they **want to*** say at the meeting?

4. How **are** you **going to** get to the station?

5. We **plan to*** buy a new computer.

6. He **is hoping to*** finish his degree by next month.

7. **Would** you **like to** meet my parents?

8. She has always **wanted to** sail around the world.

9. You won't **be able to** play football unless you have the right boots.

10. Not a lot of people **have been able to/dare to** row across the Atlantic Ocean.

11. We **had to** find a taxi because we **wanted to** get to the concert on time.

12. Do you **want to** go to a concert tonight?

13. When I was a child, I **used to** take my doll to bed with me.

14. Harold **is/isn't going to*** come to the meeting tonight.

15. Sorry, I couldn't come to your party, I **had to** go to the hospital.

*There could be several possibilities.

Negatives 221

1. We **haven't** planned our holiday yet.

2. They **haven't** been living here long.

3. The boys **cannot** go out, they **haven't** finished their homework.

4. K2 **isn't** as high as Mount Everest.

5. He plays football very well, **doesn't** he?

6. The police **didn't** think he was the murderer.

7. You **wouldn't** lie to me, would you?

8. The book **wasn't** returned to the library in time so he had to pay a fine.

9. The children **haven't** phoned their parents yet.

10. Why **didn't/don't** you come to my party?

11. I am a teacher, **aren't** I?

12. If I were you, I **wouldn't** go down that street.

13. You **mustn't** be late or you'll miss the bus.

14. She **hasn't** ever seen her father.

15. She **hasn't** been given the keys to the house so she **can't/couldn't** go in.

Negatives 222

1. The book I read last week **wasn't** interesting.

2. Albert **can't** find his shoes. Has anyone seen them?

3. There's **no** water in the pool. We **can't** swim./There **isn't** any water in the pool. We **can't** swim.

4.   **No** one's allowed to smoke in here.

5.   She **hasn't** ever forgiven her ex-boyfriend.

6.   **Not** everyone likes eating ice cream.

7.   I **won't** go to the cinema with you unless you pay for the tickets.

8.   Are you sure you **don't** want to come with us?

9.   We could climb that hill, **couldn't** we?/ We **couldn't** climb that hill, could we?

10. She **hasn't** lived here for ages.

11. You **don't** have to come if you **don't** want to.

12. You **wouldn't** happen to have $5.00, would you?

13. **Didn't** you do this exercise?

14. Brian may **not** come.

15. I **wasn't** surprised when he failed the exam.

Nouns 224

1.   His **house/car/shop**, etc., is somewhere near here.

2.   **Mary**, etc., is marrying **Peter**, etc.

3.   Andrew doesn't enjoy buying **presents** for himself.

4.   **Listening** to the radio is a good way to develop your listening skills.

5.   Do you enjoy **living** in New Zealand?

6.   Some people think **boxing**, etc., is a dangerous sport.

7.   The **house** next door has a beautiful **garden**.

8.   How old do you have to be to get a driver's **licence**?

9.   The **phone** rang just as **they** left the house.

10. The bottle was half-full of **water**, etc.

11. Turn on the TV and watch the **news**.

12. The **sun** shone through the clouds.

13. Do you know where I can find a good **book/restaurant**, etc?

14. Her garden was full of sweet-smelling **flowers**.

15. A painting in my friend's house cost a lot of **money**.

Prefixes 227

1. James missed the train because he **misread** the timetable.
2. Margaret **outlived** her husband by 10 years.
3. On Anzac Day there are **pre-dawn** parades in most towns.
4. Teams that **cooperate** are more successful than teams that don't.
5. When people are tired they can be very **impatient**.
6. Ms Jones is the **vice-principal** of my child's school.
7. These photos are very good;/ These are very good photos; we should **enlarge** them
8. Saudi Arabia is a **monotheist** country.
9. Noel's **autobiography** is very amusing.
10. **Undercooked** chicken can be very dangerous.
11. In Paris it's the metro, in London it's the **underground** and in New York it's the **subway**.
12. In ancient times, it was common practice to **enslave** the enemy.
13. The main reason for getting fat is **overeating**.
14. There are planes that can travel at **supersonic** speed.
15. The durian is a very **malodorous** fruit.

Prefixes 228

3	incorrect
4	bilingual
5	biannually
6	unpack
7	impolite
8	invisible
9	disagree
10	unemployed
11	bicycle
12	unfriendly/unsociable
13	antibiotics
14	ex-teacher

15	impatient
16	bimonthly
17	re-did
18	autopilot
19	unlike
20	dislike

21	anti-abortion
22	ex-boss
23	overheated
24	pro-government
25	pro-Cuban/pro-revolution
26	micro-computers
27	microscopic
28	mistranslated
29	misheard
30	anti-jew/jewish
31	post-graduate
32	post-revolution
33	microwave oven
34	anti-war
35	anti-government
36	misinformed
37	overeat
38	multinational
39	multipurpose
40	overslept

Suffixes 231

1. That movie **bored** me.
2. She was selected for her **beauty**.
3. We live in a very nice **neighbourhood**.
4. The doctor told him he was fine **health-wise**.
5. They went **towards** the office.
6. Most Middle-East countries have a form of **democracy**.
7. **Sailors** work on ships.

8. New Zealand is a very **picturesque** country.

9. Telecom is a multi-national **organization**.

10. Queen Street is **noisy**.

11. Are **employees** allowed to smoke in the office?

12. The **doctor** is not in at the moment, she will be here at 4.00pm.

13. What does the colour red **signify**?

14. She is an **attractive** woman?

15. He **spoke** quietly.

Prepositions 233

1. Yesterday was the hottest day yet; it was **over** 40°.

2. We haven't heard from them **since** they left New Zealand.

3. The boy kicked the ball **at (through)** the window and broke it.

4. Could you put the picture **above/below/next to** the clock **on** the wall?

5. There were some interesting trailers **before** the movie began.

6. Is the school **near/next to/close to** the bus stop?

7. He always talks **as** if he is a policeman.

8. I will only wait here **until/till** 3.00 pm.

9. The train doesn't go **beyond/(past)/to** Wellington. **From/For** Wellington you need **to** take a bus.

10. The cinema is **behind** the post office; that's why you can't see it.

11. Harriet woke up early **to** go **for** a run.

12. It's good **to** see you're **on (in)** time **for** once.

13. There were two major wars **during/in** the last century.

14. The cost **of** houses goes **up** every year.

15. They ran **away** when they saw the police.

Prepositions 234

1. A knife is **for** cutting things.

2. A friend **of** mine is a very good dancer.

3. The houses **in/on** this street are very old.

4. What do I have **to** do **to** get a visa?

5. The house was **among/next to/near/close to**, etc., the trees.

6. What is he a doctor **of**?

7. The cat was sleeping **under/on/in**, etc., the car.

8. He uses a shoebrush/hairbrush **as** a hairbrush/shoebrush.

9. Vagrants often sleep **under** the bridges **of/in** Paris.

10. What is the name **of** that hill?

11. When I asked him the question he went **off (away) in** a hurry?

12. He always goes **on** holiday **with/without** his wife.

13. Why she married him is a mystery **to** me.

14. The police asked me **to** go **over** my story again.

15. **After/Before** the movie/restaurant we went **to** a restaurant/movie.

Pronouns 237

1. Mary returned **her** books to the library; **she** had finished reading **them**.

2. **She*** and **her**** sister went on holiday together; **it** was a lot of fun.

3. Where did **you*** put the cheese? **I** can't find **it** anywhere.

4. **My**** children loved the present **I*** gave **them**; **it** gives **them** a lot of pleasure.

5. **I*** can't give **it** to **you*** it doesn't beong to **me**.

6. Albert, **who** is a maths teacher, also coaches boxing.

7. The boys were playing by **themselves** when **their** mother got home.

8. Who gave **you*** these shirts? **They** look awful!

9. This is the woman **who**se car **I** bought.

10. **My**** neighbours have decided to give a party.

11. Is this the dress **you*** would like to buy?

12. Peter is the person from **whom I*** bought **my**** golf clubs.

13. Young as **she/he** is; **she/he** can dress **herself/himself**.

14. Did **you** see **it**? **It** was very exciting, wasn't **it**?

15. **She/He** can't decide if **she/he** wants to marry **her/him** or not.

*any subject pronoun.
**any possessive pronoun
***any object pronoun

Pronouns 238

1. Jane gave **her** book to Mary.

2. **Its** colour is black.

3. Have you got **my** book?

4. Is this **mine/yours** or **yours/mine**?

5. They painted **their** house **themselves**.

6. He took **himself** off to the cinema.

7. She is always playing with **him**.

8. It's **your** book.

9. Can **I** pass it to you?

10. Which book is **yours**?

11. Did you make this doll's house **yourself**?

12. **She** can't go to the shops by **herself**, **she** is too young.

13. **I** forgot to bring **mine**, can **I** borrow **yours**?

14. **They** are very happy; **they** like **their** new house/ **They** like **their** new house; **they** are very happy.

15. **He** is always talking to **himself**.

Punctuation 239 (Opinions might vary)

1. **If the weather is fine, I'll go for a walk.***

2. **He lives in Paris.**** **He's lived there for five years.**

3. **I'm thinking of buying a new car. Do you think it's a good idea?**

4.   The **USA** is in **North America.**

5.   I don't want to go alone. **Can't you come with me?**

6.   'What a horrible man!' She said.***

7.   All the girls' shoes are on the verandah.

8.   *The Old Man and the Sea* was written by **Earnest Hemingway.**

9.   These babies' parents are from **Romania.**

10. **I**'ve lost my book. **Its** cover is blue.

11. She is a happy, cheerful, confident baby.

12. **Is** this your pen? **Do** you think **I** can borrow it?

13. **My** sister, who is a teacher, lives in **Toronto.**

14. **I**'ve seen *Blazing Saddles* many times. **It**'s a very funny movie.

15. **Some** of the things we need to buy are: cheese, bread, butter, cauliflower, etc.

16. **Of** course, all sentences begin with a capital letter and end with a full stop.

** comma, colon or semi-colon? This is a grey area.

***single or double quotations? This too is a grey area.

Punctuation 240 (same here)

1.   **Well,** the book didn't interest me at all till **I** heard a talk on the radio titled *Books,* and then **I** took notice and bought it. **It** was an interesting read.

2.   **Do** you spend a lot of time travelling?

3.   **There**'s a hotel in **Ispahan, Iran,** called **Caravanserai. The** floor in the foyer is made of a translucent material through which a soft light shines. **In** the middle there is a water fountain, in the traditional **Iranian** style. **The** water sprays upwards in the green, white and red colours of the national flag: at least, that's how **I** remember it.

4.   **Yesterday, Mary,** her sister and two friends went to the shopping mall where they bought several items of clothing: a skirt, some lipstick and a pair of stockings; then they went to the **Hoyts Cinema** and watched a film called *Pirates of the Caribbean.* **They** enjoyed it very much and thought **Johnny Depp** was really very funny.

5. **Where did they come from? O**ne minute there was no one here; the next, the place is full of people; fat, thin, **A**rabs, **I**ndians, **E**uropeans and they all seem to know each other! **W**ho are they**?**

Apostrophe 241

1. This boy's shirt is red.
2. I haven't got any pens.
3. I'm not going to see the movie *Blue Blood*. It's rubbish.
4. Those boys' boots are in the corner.
5. They've gone to Spain and won't be back till July.
6. I'd have/would've bought their house if they'd dropped the price. .
7. The teacher's/teachers' books are in this room
8. The Jones'(s) house burned down last night.
9. I couldn't have passed the exam even if I'd studied harder.
10. I'll go to the party only if Mary doesn't come.
11. I couldn't buy the car; I didn't have enough money.
12. You mustn't come late to class.
13. They're happy playing in Peter's house.
14. If they'd been invited, they'd have/would've come.
15. They won't leave until they've been paid.

Closed questions 243

1. Did you go away last weekend?
2. Can Tom drive a truck?
3. Has he got his licence yet?
4. Did you make this cake?
5. Could you wait for half an hour?
6. Were they late yesterday?
7. Have you ever fallen off a horse?
8. Was he injured in the accident?

9. Is he over twenty-five years old?

10. Would you like to go for a walk?

11. Can the children come out to play?

12. Did Peter leave on time?

13. Do they want to give a party next Saturday?

14. May I leave the office early today?

15. Will Anne be here tomorrow?

Closed questions 244

1. **Are** you **coming** to my party next Friday? **Will** you **come** to my party **next** Friday?

2. **Would** you like to **play** table tennis?/**Do** you like to **play** table tennis?/**Do** you want to **play** table tennis?

3. **Have** you ever **seen/touched/eaten**, etc., a snake?

4. **Did** I **call** the waiter?/**Shall** I call the waiter?/**Have** I **called** the waiter?/**Do** I **know** the waiter? Etc.

5. **May** I **sit** next to you?/**Can** I **sit** next to you?/**Could** I **sit** next to you?

6. **Could** you **pass/give/hand** me the butter, please? **Can** you **pass/give/hand** me the butter, please?

7. **Do** you **know** the meaning of this word?

8. **Have** you **read** the book *Don Quixote*?

9. **Do** you **like/enjoy** listening to classical music?

10. **Would** you **marry** me if I had a big house?

11. **Do I know** you?/**Do I like** you?

12. **Is** it **going to** rain tomorrow?

13. **Are** you **studying** to be a doctor?

14. **Does** she **sing** opera? **Does** she **like** opera?

15. **Would** you have **taken** the job if the salary was right?

Open questions 245

1. Who worked in a factory last year?

    What did Peter do last year?

    Where did Peter work last year?

    When did Peter work in a factory?

2. Who worked with John in a factory?

    What does Peter do?

    Who(m) does Peter work with in a factory?

    Where does Peter work?

3. Who is working with John in a factory today?

    What is Peter doing with John today?

    Who(m) is Peter working with in a factory today?

    Where is Peter working with John today?

    When is Peter working with John in a factory?

4. Which city is about 100 kms from Auckland?

    How far is Hamilton from Auckland?

    Which city is 100 kms from Hamilton?

5. Who can swim very well?

    What can Peter do very well?

    How well can Peter swim?

6. Who took his sister to school yesterday?

    What did Peter do yesterday?

    Who(m) did Peter take to school yesterday?

    Where did Peter take his sister yesterday?

    When did Peter take his sister to school?

7.   Who has bought a house?
     What has Peter done?
     What has Peter bought?

Open questions 249

1.   Which Chinese restaurant would you recommend?

2.   How many bananas can I buy for $5.00?

3.   For how long is Jonathan going to be away?

4.   Who is that person with the lovely smile?

5.   Whose car are we going in?

6.   What is the name of that animal?

7.   How much is that doggie in the window?

8.   What should I do for a headache?

9.   Which students have lost their books?

10. What colour was your car?

11. To whom did you give the ticket?

12. What are you looking at?

13. How many biscuits have you eaten?

14. What would you do if you won a million dollars?

15. Where are you going to go for your next holidays?

Open questions 250

1.   Where **were** you studying before you **came** here?

2.   What is the **best/worst** movie you **have** ever seen?

3.   **What is** the price of petrol these days?

4.   How **far** is the moon from **here**?

5.   What **can** we **buy** for $5.00?

6.   What bus **are/were** you **travelling/getting** on?

7.   **What do/would** you like to do on a nice, sunny day?

8.   **How much** did you pay for your house?

9. Which house **do/are** you **live/living** in?
10. How **did/would** you feel **when/if** you lost all your money?
11. How **much** petrol **does** your car take?
12. **Who closed/opened/broke** the window?
13. **When** is the next train **to** wellington>
14. How **long** have you **lived** in Auckland?
15. To **whom did** Andrew sell his old car?

Question with How 252

1. How **far** can a bird fly?
2. How **expensive** was your watch?
3. How **many** friends do you have?
4. How **tall** is the Sky Tower?
5. How **many** hours do you practise your English each day?
6. How **interested** are you in boxing?
7. How **exciting** was the movie you saw last night?
8. How **much** tea do you drink?
9. How **much** money do you spend each week?
10. How **often** does the Earth rotate?
11. How often **might** it rain in New Zealand?
12. How **many times** have you lost your phone?
13. How **often** have you eaten in that restaurant?
14. How **fast** can a sports car go?
15. How **long** is Queen Street?

Relative pronouns & clauses 254

1. Last year they visited a country **which** was very beautiful.
2. I remember *the* day **when** I got married.
3. The woman **whom** I met at a party was very nice.
4. They were walking in a park **where** the trees were very green.

5. We could see a man **who** was standing on his head.

6. We don't know **how** he fixed the problem.

7. He has gone back to India **where** his family is.

8. **What** he is doing, I know nothing about./I don't know anything about **what** he is doing./He is doing **what** I don't know anything about. *(convoluted, eh?)*

9. At the art gallery I was looking at a painting **that** was beautifully done.

10. This is the car **whose** owner is Bill.

11. He came to New Zealand **where** he settled happily.

12. This is his friend *for* **whom** he brought a souvenir from Cuba.

13. Saturday is the day **when** we do our grocery shopping.

14. In our school there were some children **who** didn't have any shoes.

15. I spoke to a man **who** gave me directions to the hospital.

Relative pronouns 255

1. He is *the* accountant **who** does my accounts.

2. They are *the* workmen **who** repaired our roof.

3. He is *the* racing car driver **who** won the Grand Prix last year.

4. She is my best friend *for* **whom** I bought an expensive present.

5. She is *the* artist **who** gave me a beautiful painting.

6. This is a/*the* book **which/that** has some very beautiful pictures.

7. This is my neighbour **whose** car is a Lamborghini.

8. This is the time **when** all good men must stand up and be counted

9. This is the reason **why** he can't attend the meeting.

10. A woman **who** came into the room was wearing a purple dress./A woman **who** was wearing a purple dress came into the room.

11. This is the room **where** I left my book.

12. Do you know the **man who(m)** Emma is talking **to**. Do you the man *to* **whom** Emma is talking.

13. This is the man **whose** book I borrowed.

14. These are the singers **who(m)** the company hired for three weeks./ These are the singers **who** were hired by the company for three weeks.

15. Last night I ate in a restaurant **which/that** had delicious food.

Relative pronouns 256

1. Last year they bought a house **which/that** was in the countryside.
2. I am reading a book **that/which** was written by Saki.
3. I liked the shoes (**that/which**) he was wearing at the party.
4. A car (**that/which** was) going very fast crashed into mine.
5. The book (**that** was) written by Harold is a best seller.
6. The book (**that**) she asked for was out on loan.
7. I found a letter (**that/which** was) written 200 years ago.
8. The book (**that/which**) I left on the bus belonged to the library.
9. He was the man *to* **whom** the government gave $5000./He was the man (**who(m)**) the government gave $5000 *to*.
10. He met a girl **who** invited him to a party.
11. Albert is playing badminton with a woman **who** is well-known.
12. My neighbour lives in a house **that/which** has a lot of trees around it.
13. They can't do the problem (**that/which**) you gave them yesterday.
14. The man (**who** was) playing tennis was wearing red shorts./The man (**who** was) wearing red shorts was playing tennis.
15. She gave him a book (**that/which** was/is) about Maori life in the 14th century.

Relative pronouns 257

1. This is the girl **who made her parents very happy.**
2. Those are the cars (**that were**) **made in France**.
3. Is he the man **who stole the famous painting**?
4. The elderly lady always sits **where she can see the sunset from**.

5. I'm looking forward to going on holiday **where the sun shines every day**.

6. She would like to live in a beach house **(that is) far from the city**.

7. They are going to see the movie **(that/which is) called** *The Rocky Horror Show*.

8. Margaret won a prize for her short story **(that/which was) about dogs**.

9. We bought a car **whose previous owner was a careful driver**.

10. 8.00 am is **when I catch the bus**.

11. The children are playing a computer game **(that/which) their grandmother gave them**.

12. They enjoyed the company of the woman **whose party they went to**.

13. Is this the book **(which/that) you want to buy**?

14. He was looking at a photograph of a woman **who had once been his wife**.

15. Where did you put the book **that/which has that interesting story**?

Relative pronouns 258

1. The men standing under the lamplight were plainclothes policemen.

2. The boy bouncing the ball is a good footballer.

3. The women in the black and white uniforms are world champions.

4. The dagger stolen from the museum is worth hundreds of dollars.

5. The people walking down the street have just graduated from university.

6. The book on the table has some beautiful pictures.

7. The suitcase left on the bus belonged to my uncle.

8. Can you pass me the magazine (lying) on the sofa?

9. The car parked in front of my house is a stolen car.

10. The doctors wearing blue gowns are surgeons.

11. The house built 200 years ago sold for 2 million dollars.

12. The cattle walking through the gate belong to my neighbour.

13. *The Great Gatsby*, written by F. Scott Fitzgerald, is very popular.

14. The note pinned on my door has disappeared.

15. We are going to visit the castle in Malta.

Tenses 260
Present simple & Present continuous

1. Muslims don't **eat** pork.

2. These students **read** one book a week.

3. These clothes **were** made in China.

4. Where **are** they (from)?

5. My sister and her family **are living/staying** in Canada at the moment.

6. Taxis **are** usually **driven** by immigrants.

7. **Do/Are** the police **come/coming**?/

8. The girls who **are wearing** the blue uniforms **are** very good at netball.

9. The music they **are listening/dancing** to **is** very popular.

10. The desert **gets/has** very little rain.

11. Beer **is** drunk all over the world, except in Muslim countries.

12. Some evenings I **coo**k dinner.

13. My dog doesn't **have** a tail.

14. What time **are** they **going/coming**?

15. Please **shut/close** the window; it **is** cool in here.

Tenses 261
Present simple & Present continuous

1. The sun **is shining** and the day **is** warm.

2. Religion is not **taught** in most schools.

3. They **live** in a very old house.

4. She looks lovely. She always **wears** bright colours.

5. How **do** you **go** to Hamilton? We **drive** there.

6. What **are** you **thinking** about?

7. I **am playing** tennis.

8. This TV programme **is enjoyed** by most children.

9. Those birds **are flying** into the trees.

10. The people **are waiting** outside the cinema at the moment.

11. The River Nile **flows** into the Mediterranean Sea.

12. He **is** always **sleeping** in class.

13. That woman **dresses** beautifully.

14. The librarian **is putting** the books on the shelves.

15. **Are** you **buying** this book?

Tenses 263
Past simple & Present perfect

1. It **snowed/rained** all day yesterday.

2. The house **was sold/destroyed**, etc., after the owner **left/died**, etc.

3. Lucy **got** her driving licence several months ago.

4. Paul **has sold** his old car.

5. Who **took** these photos? They are beautiful.

6. **Did** you **enjoy/like** the movie you **saw** last night?

7. My watch **was** made in Switzerland.

8. These students **were/ lived/have been/have lived** here for six months.

9. There **were** ten people in the room when the manager **came** in.

10. They **didn't** want to leave so I **phoned/ called** the police.

11. The play last night **lasted** for two hours.

12. Do you know when they **reached** the top of Mt Everest?

13. How did you **cut/hurt** your hand? It looks painful.

14. We **wore** our best clothes to the wedding.

15. No, thank you. I**'ve have** just **had** some.

Tenses 264
Past simple & Present perfect

1. She was often **mistaken** for a famous actor.
2. The little boy **hid** from his sister.
3. The wind **has swept** across the ocean.
4. I was **stung** by a bee.
5. She (gently) **laid** the child (gently) on the bed (gently).
6. These dogs were **bred** for racing.
7. She **quit** the company after an argument with her boss.
8. The alarm **has been set** for 4.00 am.
9. All through his childhood he **dreamed** of becoming a pilot.
10. The house was **destroyed** by fire.
11. The king **shook** hands with all of us.
12. The **forecast** for yesterday **was** all wrong.
13. She **has chosen** what she is going to wear.
14. The children **have** all **gone** to bed.
15. We were told to **leave** the room.

Tenses 265
Past simple & Past continuous

I **was waiting** in the doctor's surgery for my appointment when a man **entered** the room. He **was wearing** a balaclava and carrying a hammer in his left hand. I **thought** to myself, 'Don't panic.' Easier said than done. To show how calm I **was**, I **picked** up a newspaper and **pretended** to read. While I **was pretending** to read I **kept** looking over the top of the paper at the man who **was** now **sitting** by the door, staring directly in front of him. It so **happened** that I was **placed** directly in the line of his gaze. It is in moments like these that one wants to resort to comedy: two eye holes bored through the centre of the paper so I could observe him without being observed myself; for instance. Just as I **was thinking** how I **would** manage to make the holes, the doctor **entered** and **summoned** me to his room. What a relief! The doctor **didn't** mention the man in the waiting room, so neither did I. The doctor **was looking** into my ear when I **heard** a creepy sound – 'What **was** that fellow up to?'

Tenses 266
Past simple, Past continuous, Past perfect.

1.   She **didn't enjoy** the movie so she **left** before it **finished**.
2.   Steve **had** the money but he **didn't** want to give it to me.
3.   The girls **were walking/going** to the mall when they **met/saw** their parents.
4.   The flag **was raised** at dawn.
5.   A man **bumped** into me and my ice cream **fell** to the ground.
6.   He **had** just **competed/finished/written** his memoirs when he **died**.
7.   **Did** you finally buy that house? Yes, I **bought** it.
8.   The balloons **were blown** up by the children.
9.   Who **chose/bought/made**, etc., the hat with the feather on it?
10. The dictionary **was put** back on the shelf.
11. The sheep **had been killed/was eaten** by a wolf.
12. The elderly lady **burned** her lips sipping on the hot coffee.
13. They **had looked** at a lot of houses before they **found** the right one.
14. She **was withdrawing**/*taking* money *(out)* from the ATM machine when she **was robbed**.
15. The train **was coming** into the station while we **were/were eating**, etc., in the cafe.

Tenses 267
Past simple, Past continuous, Past perfect & Past continuous

1. Julia **was** at the party? What **was** she **wearing**?

2. The students **were** busily **talking** to each other when the lecturer **walked** in.

3. While our house **was being built**; we **lived** in tents.

4. I **visited** the university library yesterdeay; a lot of students **were studying** quietly.

5. We **were strolling** through the park; a dog **ran** up to us and **dropped** a ball at our feet.

6. They **decided** to take a taxi because it **was raining**.

7. They **were packing** up the tent when the earthquake **struck**.

8. While the bed **was being carried** up the stairs, the cat **ran** between our legs.

9. Herbie **hadn't been attending** classes so he **was** disqualified.

10. The statues **were being taken** to the museum when they **were stolen**.

11. While I **was sitting** by the window a bird **crashed** into it.

12. Simon **had been watching** football on TV while his children **were playing** in the yard.

13. She **was working** at her computer when I snuck up and **gave** her a fright.

14. What **were** the children **being shown**?

15. The car **had been removed** from the scene of the accident.

Name the Parts of Speech 269
These are just sample answers
1.

You	are	very	thirsty
and	would	like	to
have	a	drink.	

2.

She	is	a	writer,
she	writes	in	French.

3.

You	can't	see	the
parade	because	the	crowd
is	standing	in	front
of	you.		

4.

The	teacher	stood	up
and	walked	to	the
door.			

5.

Her	husband,	Peter,	is	handsome.

6.

We	often	drive	to
the	countryside	on	Sunday.

7.

Where	do	you	go

in	the	weekends?

8.

Peter	and	Mary	travel	in
a	very	expensive	caravan.	

9.

We	were	going	to	the	door
when	the	door- bell	rang.		

10.

While	we	were	looking	at
a	painting,	a	picture	fell
near	us.			

The Absolute End!